The *Exemplary* LEADER

The
Exemplary
LEADER

Dr. Costa S. Deir

International Leadership Seminars, Inc.
Lima, New York

Printed in the United States of America
INTERNATIONAL LEADERSHIP SEMINARS, Inc.
P.O. Box 56A
Lima, NY 14485
716-624-9660 (Tel)
716-624-9129 (Fax)

International Standard Book Number: 1-889433-00-4
Library of Congress Catalogue Card Number: 96-77831

*We dedicate this book to God
and His servants whom we
are called to serve.*

Acknowledgements

We are grateful for the help of the many who helped to make this book a reality. May the fruits of their labor be multiplied greatly for the glory of God.

Contents at a Glance

Table of Contents

LIST OF STORIES

PREFACE

The Proverbial Concepts presented in this course of Leadership Principles will awaken the mind to receive truth. They are compacted capsules of truth for personal study.

Each focused statement is easy to understand, and by its brevity, prevents monotony in the learning process. It impacts, with rich variation, at times the emotions, at times the intellect. But above all, it moves the will toward greater Christian progress.

Each principle, by its illumination, directs the personality into brighter, healthier paths of living. They modify our ways of thinking, choosing, and acting, always aiming at excellence, always moving toward higher and higher levels of maturity in Christ.

The purpose of repetition of principles in different settings is geared to impact people at different levels in the process of maturing. The repetition will touch different planes of understanding through a variety of angles and approaches. This helps to drive the point, which carries the intended truth and purpose in view. This process is much like a carpenter who keeps on hammering the same nail until it reaches its destination safely and fulfills its purpose.

INTRODUCTION

An exemplary leader is one who has reached the measure of maturity to be an example. He fully exhibits highly commendable qualities and his outstanding efficiency causes him to be greatly admired.

People of every rank and file in all nations are looking for models to emulate and for heroes to follow, for examples who will set the pace and guide the course of their lives and determine their destiny.

In the exemplary leader, people see what they ought to be and hope to become, and find support in their long journey of life through the mountains of difficulties and the rough roads of hardship. They trust to find in him undaunted courage to draw from to forge their way through the impossibilities they face.

Exemplary leaders stand strong in the face of whirling tempests of misunderstanding, remain humble in the face of accusations without retaliation, and are unmoved in the face of bitter criticism in the midst of all life's billows, while exhibiting Christ in His fullness.

An exemplary leader's commitment to excellence is unabated. His upright walk with God stirs up in others an awakening and a strong desire to follow him unquestionably. His depth of dedication provokes in others a strong inclination to become like him with unprecedented zeal and a holy determination that exceed the norm.

An exemplary leader is looked up to by man and is highly commended by God as he lives the well-pleasing life before Him. If we fail to be exemplary leaders, we fail in our leadership.

I. The NEED for Exemplary Leaders

For people to follow, they must have a leader who goes before them all the way. It is no exaggeration to say that the greatest need of the hour in every realm of life is for leaders who have matured through their years of hardships, disappointments, difficulties, accusations, failures, rejections, persecutions, misunderstandings, set backs, and everything else that the crucible can make out of them, to qualify them for their arduous role.

To become an exemplary leader a person must be tested by God in every area of his life for his promotion, be tempted of the Devil for his demotion, and be tried by people to reveal the quality of his character. He has to go through various adverse circumstances to prove him in his attitudes, actions, and reactions.

Pastor leads the way in sacrificial giving

I was laboring frequently in a country where I was invited to stay with a dear couple who continually exemplify biblical hospitality. One time when they picked me up from the airport, they explained that there is a surprise waiting for me.

Upon inquiry they stated that their missionary-minded pastor sold his house and gave the money to missions (their budget was one million US dollars). They continued saying that since he had done this, the whole church followed his sacrificial example with excitement and ecstasy. Now they had moved to a smaller apartment where they were fully contented.❏

Exemplary leaders move the hearts of their people. Example is a mighty compelling force that sets the pace for ardent followers to pursue. God give us more leaders of this caliber for millions to emulate!

Principle	Comment
1. The moral malignancy and the spiritual bankruptcy of the human race call for leaders who shine brighter than the noonday sun in the midst of gross darkness.	• We can only shine progressively brighter by being much alone with God in the secret place, being saturated with His glory and enriched by His anointing daily.

Isaiah 60:1-2 (NKJV) Arise, shine; for your light has come! And the glory of the LORD is risen upon you. {2} For behold, the darkness shall cover the earth, and deep darkness the people; but the LORD will arise over you, and His glory will be seen upon you.

---

2. People are seeking leaders who can make a difference in their lives for the best.	• The greater their consecration, the greater the difference they will make.

John 15:3 (NKJV) "You are already clean because of the word which I have spoken to you."

	Principle	*Comment*

3.   The power of example is the greatest, for it speaks the loudest and draws others to follow.

     • No argument can prevail against an example. It is a revelation of fulfilled truth.

1 Timothy 4:12,16 (NKJV)   Let no one despise your youth, but be an example to the believers in word, in conduct, in love, in spirit, in faith, in purity. {16} Take heed to yourself and to the doctrine. Continue in them, for in doing this you will save both yourself and those who hear you.

———————

4.   An exemplary leader is the greatest inspiration for others to follow.

     • Being an example, though it is costly, pays the best dividends.

John 13:14-15 (NKJV)   "If I then, your Lord and Teacher, have washed your feet, you also ought to wash one another's feet. {15} For I have given you an example, that you should do as I have done to you."

———————

Principle	*Comment*
5. The chief ministry of a leader is to lead people beyond where they are by precept and by example.	• Only leaders who are moving with God move people to God by inspiring and motivating them to action.

1 Peter 2:21 (NKJV)   For to this you were called, because Christ also suffered for us, leaving us an example, that you should follow His steps:

| 6. A leader affects people by the kind of spirit he manifests more than by the words he utters. | • The kind of spirit we have is reflected in what we are. It touches and affects people's spirit. |

Acts 6:8-10 (NKJV)   And Stephen, full of faith and power, did great wonders and signs among the people. {9} Then there arose some...disputing with Stephen. {10} And they were not able to resist the wisdom and the Spirit by which he spoke.

Principle	*Comment*

7. A pound of exemplary leadership is worth more than a ton of advice given to others.

- What people see affects them 90%—what they hear, only 10%.

Matthew 11:4-5 (NIV)   Jesus replied, "Go back and report to John what you hear and see: {5} The blind receive sight, the lame walk, those who have leprosy are cured, the deaf hear, the dead are raised, and the good news is preached to the poor.

---

8. Leaders by virtue of their position, authority, capabilities, and performance, become the example of social values for others to follow.

- The value of an exemplary leader can't be counted in terms of money; it supersedes all the currency in the world. His spiritual impact is transforming.

Psalm 78:70-72 (NKJV)   He also chose David His servant, and took him from the sheepfolds; {71} from following the ewes that had young He brought him, to shepherd Jacob His people, and Israel His inheritance. {72} So he shepherded them according to the integrity of his heart, and guided them by the skillfulness of his hands.

Principle	**Comment**
9. When Jesus said, "Follow me," it implied that the leader should take the lead, directing the way by his example and beckoning others to follow.	• Some leaders are followed; others are being chased. A leader's attitude determines the outcome. Exemplary leaders draw people while the opposite kind offends them.

Mark 1:17 (NKJV)   Then Jesus said to them, "Follow Me, and I will make you become fishers of men."

| 10. A guide points the way, but a leader leads the way for others to follow him in whatever he is doing and wherever he is going. | • It is more costly to be a leader than to be a guide, but it pays better dividends in the long run. His qualities are a compelling force. |

Hebrews 12:1-2 (NKJV)   "...{2} looking unto Jesus, the author and finisher of our faith, who for the joy that was set before Him endured the cross, despising the shame, and has sat down at the right hand of the throne of God.

II. The CHARACTERISTICS & SIGNS
of an Exemplary Leader

Characteristics & Signs
A. In relationship to GOD

It is a great responsibility for any leader to become a godly example in the midst of this wayward generation. This is the path trodden by godly men of old who proved their strong relationship with God by following circumspectly in His footsteps. The ultimate injunctions "Be holy, because I am holy." (Leviticus 11:44, niv) and "walk before Me and be blameless." (Genesis 17:1, niv) come from God Himself. "We become like the one we obey" is a universal principle for good or bad.

Tragic obedience results in addiction
In the second World War, I was a young man enamored by sports. As a Physical Training Instructor I used to train young people. When war broke out I was engaged in several professions with armies from different nations. One of the soldiers I befriended was an alcoholic. He kept urging me to drink with him. I emphatically told him that being in sports prohibited me from destroying my liver and health through drinking.

One day, he prevailed upon me to have just a sip, then another and another. If the direction of the first step in anything is wrong, we are going to end up wrong, no matter who wronged us. Being an extremist, I became addicted to alcohol in a short time. One big bottle of wine before breakfast, one before lunch, one before dinner, and at night I resorted to mixed drinking.

I was rejected by two hospitals in Jerusalem and one in Bethlehem and was sent home a hopeless case, after I spent all my savings. It was while I was in that hopeless state that I heard the Gospel and was saved and healed by Christ. Praise His Name!❏

All this tragedy was the result of obedience, but to the wrong person. Since obedience is the key to becoming what we want to be, then our obedience to God is the Grand Master Key to becoming like our Heavenly Father. Obedience shapes our life.

1. Follows the leading of the Lord

What keeps every leader safe from guessing, or copying others, or being influenced by changing circumstances, is to be led by the Holy Spirit. It is God's will that we know His will in every decision we make in order to fulfill His eternal purpose. Leaders who have a heart that seeks after God are attentive to His voice and sensitive to His leadings. "And ye shall seek me, and find me, when ye shall search for me with all your heart." (Jeremiah 29:13, kjv) Herein lies our safety as well as the safety of the whole operation we are responsible for.

Two leaders reconciled, a continent saved

One day as I was seeking the Lord, the Spirit of the Lord spoke to me saying "Fly immediately to a certain country where two leaders are having a bitter dispute. Their lives have been affecting a whole continent through their combined ministry." I phoned, communicated with both of them and shared what the Lord had spoken to me. They consented to my coming.

When they met me at the airport, we went to one of their homes for a preliminary session. With each passing moment tension was mounting high between the two men. When we arrived at the home where I was staying there was a volcanic eruption between them. Tension unresolved becomes contention, so I canceled the meeting immediately and made an appointment with them for the next morning.

Most of the night I was in tears of intercession with groaning, travailing, and sighing. I was doing battle in the Heavenly realm with demonic forces who had succeeded in bringing division between two leaders who once moved as one in a mighty ministry.

It is amazing what we can do for the Lord if we are not seeking credit. However we do know that God keeps accurate accounts. Where there is immaturity, insecurity, selfishness, pride, and rebellion, there are bound to be divisions that will lead to disaster. We met the next day and after hearing both sides I sought the Lord for the truth. There are always three sides to every story.

The Spirit of the Lord descended upon me. It was a mighty and rich anointing that lasted for three hours. The Word of the Lord was flowing, unveiling the causes of the division, and the stratagem of Satan and his plan to destroy them. This would cause millions of people who knew them to stumble. The presence of the Lord descended mightily on both of them and began to melt their hearts. The tears began to flow and hardened hearts became tender.

I asked one brother to go and bring some water and a towel, which he did. I said, "Please wash your brother's feet while you pray for him." There was a slight hesitancy, but then he moved swiftly and did exactly what I asked him to do. I asked the other brother to lay hands on his head and pray for him in the mean-time. Both men were sobbing. After a while I asked them to change positions and their personal revival continued to burst forth from the throne of God.

They could take it no more. They hugged and kissed each other for a long time. They asked forgiveness and confessed their sins to the Lord. Suddenly there was a great outburst of joy. The Spirit of the Lord melted their hearts together and once again they felt that divine surgery had been performed successfully.

After lunch we flew to one of the largest cities in their country to minister in one of its largest churches. That night the Holy Spirit fell. The presence of God was manifested mightily. Many received the Holy Spirit with power. Revival was moving in full force. Glory be to God.❏

It pays to be attentive to the voice of the Lord, to be sensitive to His leading, and to be prompt in obeying Him.

Principle	*Comment*
11. Jesus went about doing good, meeting the needs of people—no wonder the Bible says, "the world has gone after him." Blessed is the leader who follows in his master's steps.	• We manifest Christ most in our depth of service to others. The greater a leader's role, the greater his service to others should be. Depth of service to others is the trademark of being an example.

John 12:19 (NKJV)   The Pharisees therefore said among themselves, "You see that you are accomplishing nothing. Look, the world has gone after Him!"

---

12. The example of Christ should be the pattern of life for every leader who desires is to be an under-shepherd.	• Everyone emulates his hero—regardless of his age or stage. Christ's dynamic example is the mightiest transforming force on earth.

John 10:11 (NIV)   "I am the good shepherd. The good shepherd lays down his life for the sheep."

Principle	**Comment**
13. A leader who is born of God must certainly resemble his Father to attract people to Him.	• "We become like the one we obey" is a universal law. Every act of obedience to God changes us into His likeness.

John 10:30 (NKJV)   Jesus answered them,... "I and My Father are one."...

---

14. Leaders who live close to the Lord reflect Him best and exhibit His glory.	• As the moon reflects the sun, so leaders must be divine reflectors.

Acts 4:13 (NKJV)   Now when they saw the boldness of Peter and John, and perceived that they were uneducated and untrained men, they marveled. And they realized that they had been with Jesus.

Principle	*Comment*
15. Leaders ought to walk circumspectly with God for their own sakes and for the sake of those whose eyes are upon them.	• The greater the role, the greater and more serious the accountability will be. We bless many when we are examples, but we offend and stumble many when we are not.

Ephesians 5:14-16 (NKJV)   Therefore He says: "Awake, you who sleep, arise from the dead, and Christ will give you light." {15} See then that you walk circumspectly, not as fools but as wise, {16} redeeming the time, because the days are evil.

| 16. The more a leader gives his life to the cause of his Master, the more his followers will emulate him. | • Leaders must pass three tests in life to be real examples: loving, giving, and forgiving. |

Galatians 1:3-4 (NKJV)   Grace to you and peace from God the Father and our Lord Jesus Christ, {4} who gave Himself for our sins, that He might deliver us from this present evil age, according to the will of our God and Father,

---

Principle	**Comment**
17. A leader who is inspired by the Holy Spirit in his walk with God, has super motivating power to reach his highest goal.	• The stronger our inspiration, and the greater our motivation, the faster we will reach our set goal with rest in our spirit.

Philippians 3:12 (NKJV)   Not that I have already attained, or am already perfected; but I press on, that I may lay hold of that for which Christ Jesus has also laid hold of me.

———————

18. The leader who is enamored by Christ's example has determined what he wants to become by the grace of God.	• We become what we aim for. Our decisions have a far-reaching effect with eternal consequences.

1 John 2:6 (NKJV)   He who says he abides in Him ought himself also to walk just as He walked.

———————

2. Manifests and glorifies Christ

Only when a leader manifests Christ in whatever he thinks, says, and does, does he glorify the Lord. A leader's first calling is to exemplify Christ who desires to find expression in his mortal body (2 Corinthians 4:10-11). The Lord affords leaders ample opportunities to manifest Him through all the contrarinesses of life He allows them to go through. All opposition, accusations, criticism, misunderstandings, and failures, are means and opportunities to help leaders blossom with the fruit of the Spirit and glorify God in their behavior.

Soldier's hard heart melted by love

In a country where Christians are greatly persecuted, a soldier was torturing one of the Christian leaders. In this country persecution could be imprisonment and torture to the point of death. While the soldier was torturing the Christian leader, he became exhausted from beating him and took an intermission. During the break he asked him the question, "Why don't you recant and save your life? You are being beaten to death and you still insist on loving Jesus. What can Jesus do for you now?"

His reply was quick, "Jesus gave me much love for you while you were beating me. He asked me to forgive you and pray for your salvation."

The soldier saw his victim bleeding, maligned, persecuted unmercifully, and yet oozing with the love of Christ with the unexpected reply of "Jesus gave me love to forgive you and pray for your salvation." Such words were irresistible to the soldier. They were anointed by the Holy Spirit. It pierced the heart of the soldier who knelt down immediately and asked the Christian leader to forgive him. He then asked him to lead him to Christ. The Christian was quick to do just that. It was a glorious climax that magnified Christ and glorified the Lord God our Father.❏

	Principle	*Comment*

19. The greatest leader is the one whose life always points to Christ.

- His godly life exemplifies Christ and makes him most effective.

John 12:21 (NKJV) Then they came to Philip, who was from Bethsaida of Galilee, and asked him, saying, "Sir, we wish to see Jesus."

---

20. The leader who is a godly example manifests Christ in his motives, attitudes, actions, and reactions.

- Total manifestation of Christ is required from exemplary leaders whose aim is to glorify the Lord and exalt His Name.

2 Corinthians 2:14 (NKJV) Now thanks be to God who always leads us in triumph in Christ, and through us diffuses the fragrance of His knowledge in every place.

---

21. Some leaders say, "Follow me"; others say, "Follow me, as I follow Christ"; what a great difference, with results that are obvious to all.

- No leader has the right to a following unless he is ardently following Christ. That's what makes following him safe and fruitful.

1 Corinthians 11:1 (NIV) Follow my example, as I follow the example of Christ.

Principle	*Comment*

22. When Christ's love enriches a leader's life, it brings forth Christ's likeness in full expression.

• The greater the love, the closer the likeness. Love is the mightiest transforming power.

John 13:34 (NKJV)   "A new commandment I give to you, that you love one another; as I have loved you, that you also love one another."

---

23. When a leader's attitudes and actions are conspicuously righteous, they reflect the character of our Lord Jesus Christ, who is the source and standard of righteousness.

• Blessed is the leader who manifests Christ's characteristics in fullness. He gives a true revelation of what God is like. God desires to be personified and exemplified in His leaders.

1 Peter 1:16 (NKJV)   because it is written, "Be holy, for I am holy."

	Principle	*Comment*

24.   The most shining examples among leaders are those who exhibit holy character and righteous judgment.

• Holy character is the best reflection of God. Holiness is God's nature, while righteousness is His character.

2 Corinthians 7:1 (NKJV)   Therefore, having these promises, beloved, let us cleanse ourselves from all filthiness of the flesh and spirit, perfecting holiness in the fear of God.

---

25.   Every earnest leader must have a true revelation of who Jesus is, if he is to represent Him and lead others under His Lordship.

• Beholding Him we are changed to change others. What affects a leader automatically affects his followers as well and to the same extent.

Galatians 1:15-16 (NKJV)   But when it pleased God, who separated me from my mother's womb and called me through His grace, {16} to reveal His Son in me, that I might preach Him among the Gentiles, I did not immediately confer with flesh and blood,

Principle	*Comment*
26. An exemplary leader is known by the risks he takes, the decisions he makes, and the tasks he fearlessly undertakes for the glory of God.	• Leaders become examples by forging their way through to the forefront with faces like a flint and boldness of faith.

Exodus 14:13 (NKJV)   And Moses said to the people, "Do not be afraid. Stand still, and see the salvation of the LORD, which He will accomplish for you today. For the Egyptians whom you see today, you shall see again no more forever."

---

27. An exemplary leader's behavior should not be determined by the mis-behavior of others, but should reflect the qualities of Christ.	• The mature life of a leader reflects the full-ness of Christ both in smooth and contrary circumstances in life.

2 Corinthians 10:12 (NKJV)   For we dare not class ourselves or compare ourselves with those who commend themselves. But they, measuring themselves by themselves, and comparing themselves among themselves, are not wise.

Principle	**Comment**
28. Good leaders go about doing good like their master, while others just go about.	• Leaders who refuse to pay the price for living the good news are bad news and a bad influence.

Acts 10:38 (NKJV)   "...God anointed Jesus of Nazareth with the Holy Spirit and with power, who went about doing good and healing all who were oppressed by the devil, for God was with Him."

3. Studies and lives by Christ's principles

Leaders who are ardent students of the Scriptures are enriched by divine principles that guide their lives on the path of fulfillment and satisfaction in their walk with God. Some leaders live by expediencies or by what they consider convenient in every circumstance and end up in disappointment. Only lives guided by divine principles will come up to the standard that pleases God and has His approval. Divine principles protect leaders from outside influences that invade their lives from every segment of society.

Shop owner shocked by high standards

A leader is now pastoring a church just outside Jerusalem. While in training, he was also working in a TV and radio repair shop to support his family. The owner of the TV shop was greatly pleased with his diligence and conscientiousness.

One day the owner of the shop asked him to lie, saying, "I will be gone to the city of Jerusalem to do some business. If some customers come, have them wait here. Tell them I am working inside on an urgent job and I will soon be out."

To the owner's surprise, the answer was, "Sir, I cannot lie. That is against the principles of God that I live by. I must be honest and truthful and upright before God and before man." The owner of the shop was shocked. He had never met anybody with convictions like that. He said to him, "I am greatly pleased with your diligence, with your work, and with your attendance in coming and going to work. But even more than that, I am pleased that you do not steal money from the shop. I am only asking you to do one thing, just to lie so I will not lose any customers."

He repeated his convictions very politely, but emphatically. The owner said, "The fellows who worked here before you were willing to lie when I asked them to do so. They were also stealing from me. That is why I let them go. You don't steal, but you will not lie. A lie doesn't cost you anything." He said, "Yes, it costs me my relationship with God. God is truth and truthful. To walk with God requires that I be truthful at all times and in all ways, for I live in the presence of God."

The owner of the store threatened him that he would have no job the next day if he insisted on not following his orders to lie to the customers. He said to him, "Don't wait until tomorrow, I will leave right now." The man was greatly puzzled and at the same time he was touched by meeting a man who lives by the highest standard that he had ever heard—by applying divine principles. To say the least, he was affected.❑

Every test we go through in life is basically a test of honesty. We should read Psalm 139 daily (see Appendix C). This gives us the revelation of the omnipresence of God, the omnipotence of God, and the omniscience of God.

Principle	*Comment*

29. The most spiritual leader is the most practical; he applies God's principles in his daily life through the power of the Holy Spirit.

• Applying God's principles leads one up to God's standard, where he finds the pleasure and the approval of God. What God proves He approves.

Acts 6:3 (NKJV)   "Therefore, brethren, seek out from among you seven men of good reputation, full of the Holy Spirit and wisdom, whom we may appoint over this business;"

---

30. The leader who is fully determined to give himself wholly to a lifetime of studying and living by God's principles, exemplifies his Lord and influences people most by his dynamic resourcefulness.

• Determination does not hesitate to pay any price to fulfill its purpose. It demonstrates a depth of love and relationship. It stems out of a deep commitment to excellence.

2 Timothy 2:15 (NKJV)   Be diligent to present yourself approved to God, a worker who does not need to be ashamed, rightly dividing the word of truth.

Principle	**Comment**

31. The leader who starts the day with an open Bible will reflect its contents all day long in his life for the simplest people to read.

- Being enriched by truth rewards a leader with greater efficiency to touch lives. When truth is fully imbibed it produces the qualities of Christ.

Psalm 19:7 (NKJV)   The law of the LORD is perfect, converting the soul; the testimony of the LORD is sure, making wise the simple;

---

32. The leader who feeds his mind with the Bread of Life will find God's truth transforming his being and bringing him into mature manhood, where Christ can be fully expressed.

- Yielding to the Holy Spirit through His instructions, wooings, and gracious leadings in the minute details that matter most, brings us to full maturity, which brings fulfillment in life.

2 Timothy 3:15-16 (NKJV)   and that from childhood you have known the Holy Scriptures, which are able to make you wise for salvation through faith which is in Christ Jesus. {16} All Scripture is given by inspiration of God, and is profitable for doctrine, for reproof, for correction, for instruction in righteousness,

---

Principle	*Comment*

33.   A leader who is an illumi-   • A glowing example shines
      nating Biblical example in   farther than the sun at
      his walk with God, bright-   noonday. The more we are
      ens the road for others to   filled with truth the far-
      follow.   ther we shine like a flood
                                        light.

Proverbs 4:18 (NKJV)   But the path of the just is like the
shining sun, that shines ever brighter unto the perfect day.

34.   A lively leader makes the   • The Bible was given to us
      Bible alive by living it.   not to be viewed, but to be
                                        lived.

James 1:22 (NKJV)   But be doers of the word, and not
hearers only, deceiving yourselves.

B. In relationship to OTHERS

A leader who desires to influence the lives and walk of others must live far beyond where his followers are for them to see his godly example and the high price he's willing to pay regardless of what he has to go through. Jesus, who was our highest example, was reviled but reviled not. He inspires the same in us.

Proud teacher repays commendation with criticism

I was asked to recommend a teacher to lecture in a Bible school in a foreign country where I had taught for several years. I highly recommended a brother whom I had helped to hold a high position in an institution without knowing much about his character. I asked that they pay his return ticket and an honorarium as a gesture of love, and they consented.

After he fulfilled his assignment, I happened to pass through that country. To my shock, my close friends were angry with me. Upon inquiring, they said "you spoke well of this brother and commended him highly and for two weeks all he did was speak against you and degrade you, and even criticized your hospitality, which we know to be first class, for we have been in your home."

I was shocked and tried to brush it off and comfort them. He and I were friends and I never had anything against him, and anytime he needed help I would respond gladly. They offered to give me the tapes to hear what he had to say. The Lord prevented me from doing so and said, "I reviled not—will you follow my example?" "Absolutely, Lord!"

Upon coming back, he and I were supposed to be on the same board of an institution. Half way through a business meeting he showed up and searched for a seat, but there was none except the seat beside me. He was a nervous wreck, restless all the time. I greeted him with my customary hug and kiss.

At some juncture in the business meeting, he asked me if I had visited the country where he lectured. I replied that I just came back from there. From that moment on he gave me more of his back than his face. As soon as the meeting was over, he shot out of there faster than lightening.

I asked what kind of behavior he exhibits among his new colleagues. The reply was, "he's critical of everybody. His pride and self-righteous attitude compel him to shred everyone he can, unsparingly."❑

Immaturity and insecurity plague some leaders who develop their ministry but neglect the development of their character, which is the foundation.

Principle	*Comment*
35. A leader's greatest asset is the example he sets before his subordinates; it illuminates their eyes to follow him.	• Leaders who are assets produce the same kind of followers. God deliver us from leaders who are liabilities.

1 Timothy 4:12 (NKJV)   Let no one despise your youth, but be an example to the believers in word, in conduct, in love, in spirit, in faith, in purity.

Principle	**Comment**
36. Every leader needs to become a model to be seen before he can become an example to be followed.	• People are affected more by what they see than by what they hear. Seeing is far more convincing and effective.

1 Peter 3:15-16 (NKJV)   But sanctify the Lord God in your hearts, and always be ready to give a defense to everyone who asks you a reason for the hope that is in you, with meekness and fear; {16} having a good conscience, that when they defame you as evildoers, those who revile your good conduct in Christ may be ashamed.

———————————

| 37. A leader must be genuine to qualify for being an example for others to follow. | • Superficiality reveals an empty shell that has nothing to offer. |

Romans 12:16 (NKJV)   Be of the same mind toward one another. Do not set your mind on high things, but associate with the humble. Do not be wise in your own opinion.

———————————

Principle	*Comment*

38. A leader who is an original will stand far above the shoulders of many, especially in these days of superficiality.

• A secure leader is stable and real, not a copyist. The best copy is still a copy. No matter what the cost of being a realist, dare to be one.

Galatians 1:11-12 (NKJV)   But I make known to you, brethren, that the gospel which was preached by me is not according to man. {12} For I neither received it from man, nor was I taught it, but it came through the revelation of Jesus Christ.

---

39. An exemplary leader communicates his qualities to his people by the life he lives, not just by the precepts he teaches.

• Life lived aright brings the right results. It paves the way for others to follow. He who has the light is entitled to lead the way.

John 13:15 (NIV)   I have set you an example that you should do as I have done for you.

---

1. Motivates and stimulates others by his example

Leaders who fail to inspire their people by their example will fail to stimulate their interest and will not be able to motivate them into action. An exemplary leader is alive, vibrant. and most challenging to all who observe his walk and performance. He stirs up in others the same desire that is burning in his heart. His vision is contagious, his zeal and steadfastness of faith ignite divine fire and power in his followers.

A lesson in motivation from the car

I was invited to address a leadership conference in one of the richest nations in the world. This was the only conference of that type I have ever attended. The conference speaker addresses the group once in the morning. The afternoon is spent studying everything he said, word by word. The evening session is set aside to question the speaker on everything he said in the morning session. It was then I discovered that every time we open our mouth, we are on trial.

One of the questions was "Why are we failing to motivate our people to serve the Lord?" It is a common question the world over. Time and again I have had leaders pick me up from the airport in different nations telling me, "I am pastoring a church in the hardest place in the world. My people are hard to motivate. It is hard to get them to do anything for God. We are in a state of stagnation. I trust God sent you to help us."

My question to the man was, "Have you ever been outside the country?" "No." "How do you know that God put you in the hardest place in the world?" This is the assumption of a defeated leader who is not in vital contact with the Throne daily. My answer to the leader who asked the question was, "I will answer you, if you first answer my question." That is the way Jesus responded to people's questions.

So I commenced by saying, "Have you ever seen anybody sitting in a car, moving the steering wheel from right to left all day long and pushing the accelerator continually without starting the engine?" He exclaimed in a loud voice, "Of course not!" I said, "You answered right and answered your own question."

In everything we do, unless we take our first step in the right direction, our second step is liable to be in the wrong direction.

You cannot motivate a person unless you first inspire him. You cannot expect the car to move by pushing the accelerator unless you first start the engine. Failure to inspire others results in failure to motivate them. A leader must know how to inspire, how to motivate, and how to challenge his people to continue accelerating until they reach the goal.

To inspire means to sow a seed of thought or an idea where there has been none. To inspire means to impart a vision, to instill a goal, to awaken in a person a new desire towards greatness. Once a person has been inspired, it is easy to motivate him to action.❏

Principle	*Comment*
40. An exemplary leader is the best person to emulate and the most inspiring person to follow.	• A shining example has an unseen force that propels him. He is endowed with rich anointing, which makes him vibrant and full of vitality.

1 Timothy 4:12 (NKJV)   Let no one despise your youth, but be an example to the believers in word, in conduct, in love, in spirit, in faith, in purity.

| 41. Jesus said, "I am the way" and an exemplary leader becomes the way for others to follow. | • Millions are waiting for exemplary leaders to lead so they can follow confidently. |

John 14:6 (NKJV)   Jesus said to him, "I am the way, the truth, and the life. No one comes to the Father except through Me."

| 42. An exemplary leader provokes people to goodness and attracts them to move in the direction of his set goal. | • Directed people are powerful in their pursuit. They are saved from distractions and from detours. |

Hebrews 10:24 (NKJV)   And let us consider one another in order to stir up love and good works,

---

Principle	*Comment*
43. Every move a leader makes and word he speaks reflect his goals, consciously or unconsciously.	• Unless a leader is obsessed with his goal, he will never reach it, and will not be able to transmit it to others.

Matthew 12:35 (NKJV)   "A good man out of the good treasure of his heart brings forth good things, and an evil man out of the evil treasure brings forth evil things."

---

44. Whatever a leader does gives others the ideas that motivate them, because their eyes are upon him.	• Inspired ideas whose time for fulfillment has come, make all the difference in a leader's life and in his people.

Nehemiah 2:18 (NKJV)   And I told them of the hand of my God which had been good upon me, and also of the king's words that he had spoken to me. So they said, "Let us rise up and build." Then they set their hands to this good work.

Principle	**Comment**
45. Harmony demands sacrifice from the whole group. The leader must lead the way to inspire in others what is in him.	• Harmony is most essential to great achievements; where harmony prevails unity is enjoyed, leading to greater productivity.

1 Peter 3:8 (NIV)   Finally, all of you, live in harmony with one another; be sympathetic, love as brothers, be compassionate and humble.

| 46. The leader who is willing to tackle tough assignments joyfully, will impart confidence in his subordinates to perform their best. | • Leaders who move joyfully and confidently are able to tackle the toughest tasks, fully assured of astounding results. |

1 Peter 4:12-13 (NKJV)   Beloved, do not think it strange concerning the fiery trial which is to try you, as though some strange thing happened to you; {13} but rejoice to the extent that you partake of Christ's sufferings, that when His glory is revealed, you may also be glad with exceeding joy.

---

2. Affects his followers for Christ

Leaders whose lives are affected by living close to Christ will affect their followers to that same measure for Christ. A life that overflows with His life enjoys an unprecedented gush of blessings that touches many lives for God. The fullness of Christ awaits our emptiness.

Training the younger generation to assume greater responsibility in gathering the harvest worldwide is most exciting and rewarding. During the past forty-eight years, I have trained young people in pastoring churches and ministered in Bible colleges in many parts of the world. I have also trained potential leaders in leadership seminars on every continent.

As I continue to travel I meet many people in different nations who have been trained under our ministry and are now fully engaged in effective ministry for the Lord. Obeying the call of God brings fulfillment to His will.

The ministry has impacted their lives. It has stirred them up for the work of God. It has released the fire of God in their hearts with a rich anointing to move swiftly to help in gathering the harvest. It is most exhilarating to meet these people in so many places and hear their reports. It is encouraging to affect people's lives for Christ. To God be all the glory.

Pastors need to convert their churches to training centers to produce harvesters for the end times, to gather in the whitened fields worldwide.

Principle	*Comment*
47. The first calling of a leader is to manifest Christ to his colleagues, as well as to his followers. Failure in this area means a disastrous end.	• He who aims the highest and pays the price, is bound to get there on time. Enjoying the dividends makes a leader forget the price, no matter how high it has been.

Galatians 4:19 (NKJV)   My little children, for whom I labor in birth again until Christ is formed in you,

---

48. The leader who lives close to God reflects His beauty wherever he goes and brightens the lives of others.	• Our receptivity to God enriches our lives with His characteristics and helps us to radiate them farthest.

2 Corinthians 4:6 (NKJV)   For it is the God who commanded light to shine out of darkness, who has shone in our hearts to give the light of the knowledge of the glory of God in the face of Jesus Christ.

Principle	**Comment**
49. The leader who lives close to God usually helps people do likewise, for his example is the greatest drawing card.	• The closer a leader lives to God the more magnetic he becomes in helping draw people to the Lord by his life and the way he conducts himself.

Psalms 51:10-13 (NIV)   Create in me a pure heart, O God, and renew a steadfast spirit within me. {11} Do not cast me from your presence or take your Holy Spirit from me. {12} Restore to me the joy of your salvation and grant me a willing spirit, to sustain me. {13} Then I will teach transgressors your ways, and sinners will turn back to you.

———————

50. A leader who enjoys a healthy relationship with God produces healthy followers who live close to Him.	• A healthy relationship with God is the foundation on which to build a fruitful life.

John 15:5 (NKJV)   "I am the vine, you are the branches. He who abides in Me, and I in him, bears much fruit; for without Me you can do nothing."

———————

	Principle	**Comment**

51. A leader who is moving by the Spirit provokes people to arise and walk more seriously with God.

- Nothing worthwhile can be accomplished until leaders and followers become serious.

Luke 11:1 (NKJV)   Now it came to pass, as He was praying in a certain place, when He ceased, that one of His disciples said to Him, "Lord, teach us to pray, as John also taught his disciples."

---

52. As our Lord was the full revelation and expression of God the Father on earth, so should a leader be in his exemplary life.

- The more a vessel is broken, the greater will be the release of its treasure. The preciousness of the vessel is in what it contains.

John 14:9 (NKJV)   Jesus said to him, "Have I been with you so long, and yet you have not known Me, Philip? He who has seen Me has seen the Father; so how can you say, 'Show us the Father'?"

	Principle	*Comment*
53.	The leader who believes that no one lives unto himself, but is bound up in the welfare and the well-being of the whole creation of God, becomes a perpetual blessing where God's abundant life flows through him to exhibit God's glory.	• "None of us lives to himself" is a scriptural injunction that delivers us from the sin of selfishness. We are ordained of God to be channels of His grace. The purer the channel the greater the flow. Vessels of honor honor God by yielding to Him unreservedly.

Romans 14:7 (NKJV)   For none of us lives to himself, and no one dies to himself.

54.	As the salt of the earth and the light of the world, a leader must have a worldwide influence, exemplifying Christ in his life, and transmitting it to others.	• For a leader to shine he has to burn. The element of self-sacrifice must be the most evident virtue in every leader's life. The measure of our love determines the measure of our sacrifice.

Matthew 5:14 (NKJV)   "You are the light of the world. A city that is set on a hill cannot be hidden."

Principle	Comment
55. A leader who misses an opportunity to reveal Christ to friend or foe, misses one of the greatest opportunities in life to succeed.	• Christ is risen only in the lives of leaders who have died to themselves and to the things of the world. Living for Christ releases His divine qualities.

Matthew 5:44 (NKJV)   "But I say to you, love your enemies, bless those who curse you, do good to those who hate you, and pray for those who spitefully use you and persecute you,"

3. Leads by being a godly example

Holy leaders make the best godly examples. Their radiance attracts people to Christ; their walk draws people to follow Him all the way; their love melts hard hearts. Their aspiration is to represent God; their strong desire is to serve Him. They glory in His Name; they live to extol Him, worship and adore Him hilariously, and revel in His sweet presence.

Nine year old dying boy is not afraid to die

It was in a godly family that little John grew up—where love was in abundance, where joy was the normal prevailing atmosphere. His parents were affectionate and demonstrated godly characteristics.

A day came when John became deathly sick with an incurable disease. His parents did all they knew to do. Yet his condition worsened as the days went by. The day came when the family doctor advised them to take John home from the hospital, as he was near death.

While at home, John displayed a joyful confidence, a calmness in his spirit that was unprecedented. While his father was sitting beside his bed observing all of this, he asked John if he was afraid to die. John's astonishing reply was, "Dad, if God is as loving as you are, why should I be afraid to die?"❏

God give us more exemplary fathers who exhibit divine agape love that assures their children of their destiny.

Principle	**Comment**
56. An exemplary leader knows that the most valuable gift he can give is to be a godly example for others to follow.	• If one cannot be an example, he cannot be a successful leader. Shunning the price impedes his development.

2 Thessalonians 3:7-9 (NKJV)   For you yourselves know how you ought to follow us, for we were not disorderly among you; {8} nor did we eat anyone's bread free of charge, but worked with labor and toil night and day, that we might not be a burden to any of you, {9} not because we do not have authority, but to make ourselves an example of how you should follow us.

57. The first and greatest item on the list of requirements for leadership is to be a godly and ardent example of what his followers ought to be.	• Godliness is the basic lifestyle for a true leader that guarantees godly followers—who will labor with him relentlessly with joyful willingness and exciting readiness.

Titus 2:11-12 (NIV)   For the grace of God that brings salvation has appeared to all men. {12} It teaches us to say "No" to ungodliness and worldly passions, and to live self-controlled, upright and godly lives in this present age,

Principle	Comment
58. A godly leader knows that being an example is a way of life, not something extra to be put on, so he endeavors to live his best daily for God.	• Leaders who regard Christ's life as supreme, yield to His inflow and outflow, unreservedly. That is the life that glorifies God the most.

Luke 9:23 (NIV)   Then he said to them all: "If anyone would come after me, he must deny himself and take up his cross daily and follow me."

Principle	Comment
59. A godly leader walks in the fear of the Lord, realizing that the people he leads are a replica of his own lifestyle.	• The fear of the Lord teaches valuable and necessary lessons, and safeguards a leader from many pitfalls.

Proverbs 14:27 (NKJV)   The fear of the LORD is a fountain of life, to turn one away from the snares of death.

Principle	*Comment*
60. A leader who lives a holy life, rather than just talking about it, will impart the same to others.	• Holy living glitters brightly for others to see, for it radiates the presence of God.

1 Thessalonians 1:5-7 (NKJV)   For our gospel did not come to you in word only, but also in power, and in the Holy Spirit and in much assurance, as you know what kind of men we were among you for your sake. {6} And you became followers of us and of the Lord, having received the word in much affliction, with joy of the Holy Spirit, {7} so that you became examples to all in Macedonia and Achaia who believe.

---

61. An accountable leader is precise and is an example of godliness.	• Awareness of God's presence and purpose is the key to godliness, releasing God's virtues.

2 Corinthians 5:10 (NKJV)   For we must all appear before the judgment seat of Christ, that each one may receive the things done in the body, according to what he has done, whether good or bad.

Principle	**Comment**
62. Jesus said, "I left you an example to follow." As He showed His disciples Himself as a pattern, effective leaders should do likewise.	• God helps leaders to leave more than the words they speak, and more than the stories and illustrations they share. A godly life is the most powerful example to give.

1 Peter 2:20-23 (NKJV)   ...But when you do good and suffer, if you take it patiently, this is commendable before God. {21} For to this you were called, because Christ also suffered for us, leaving us an example, that you should follow His steps: {22} "Who committed no sin, nor was deceit found in His mouth"; {23} who, when He was reviled, did not revile in return; when He suffered, He did not threaten, but committed Himself to Him who judges righteously;

Principle	*Comment*
63. A leader on fire for God should excite his people by his words, example, and disposition, more than a ball game of the most famous team.	• The more fervent a leader is, the more effective he is. Where there is fire in the heart, there is power in the life. We must watch our spiritual temperature daily.

Nehemiah 2:17-18 (NKJV) Then I said to them, "You see the distress that we are in, how Jerusalem lies waste, and its gates are burned with fire. Come and let us build the wall of Jerusalem, that we may no longer be a reproach." {18} And I told them of the hand of my God which had been good upon me, and also of the king's words that he had spoken to me. So they said, "Let us rise up and build." Then they set their hands to this good work.

64. The leader who lives in a state of continual revival enjoys his people and makes them thirsty for the water of life.	• Revival should be the normal atmosphere of leaders and the church, starting in their homes. Some leaders need revival; others need resurrection.

John 4:14 (NKJV) "but whoever drinks of the water that I shall give him will never thirst. But the water that I shall give him will become in him a fountain of water springing up into everlasting life."

Principle	**Comment**
65. The consistent example of a godly leader is a sustaining inspiration to his followers on their journey to greater accomplishments.	• When a leader lives consistently in the secret place with God, he becomes resourceful and a great inspiration to others.

John 13:15 (NIV)   I have set you an example that you should do as I have done for you.

4. Leads by being an outstanding example

A leader who stands out in his character qualities as well as in his gifted performance is bound to be followed all the way. People willingly follow a leader who knows where he is going and how to get there.

Church takeover attempt backfires

I had the privilege of holding a conference in a very large, newly built church. Something happened between the pastor and two major contributors who were on the church board. They disagreed regarding a certain aspect in the church.

The two rich brethren, who were venturing to preach, thought they could take over the church and sway the people to discard their leader. It backfired on them. All the people followed the pastor. However, the two were able to take the church building back because they were the major contributors.

The men and the pastor should have set some special times aside to seek the Lord with fasting and prayer. They should have waited on the Lord for His answer. They should have consulted with more mature, more experienced leaders in the community.

The sufferings and disappointments were great. The pastor and congregation had to seek a place to meet after this confrontation. Eventually they were able to build their own church building and meet regularly.

It is possible for a person to be a good preacher, but not a good leader. The making of a preacher is less costly than the making of a leader. There is a vast difference between the two.

The two businessmen could not rally people to come to their meetings. They eventually sold the church to a school.❑

Preaching does not make examples. Godly living does. Some leaders succeed by what they know. Some succeed by what they do. A few of them succeed by what they are, which matters most.

Principle	*Comment*
66. The leader who is dedicated to quality production, inspires the same in his people by his example.	• Exemplary leaders strive for the highest in God, not considering the cost. The greatest price fades away in comparison to the supreme sacrifice.

Ecclesiastes 9:10 (NKJV)   Whatever your hand finds to do, do it with your might;...

---

67. The quality of a leader is reflected in his people and in what they produce.	• What a leader imparts, his people imbibe. They will fully express the same quality.

Acts 4:13-31 (NKJV)   Now when they saw the boldness of Peter and John, and perceived that they were uneducated and untrained men, they marveled. And they realized that they had been with Jesus....

Principle	*Comment*
68. Like leaders, like followers; as followers develop like their leaders they become a true replica, revealing the efficiency of the leadership.	• Each one produces after his own kind. Life produces life; it produces fruit in all seasons. A leader must become what he hopes to produce in his people.

2 Corinthians 3:2-3 (NKJV) You are our epistle written in our hearts, known and read by all men; {3} clearly you are an epistle of Christ, ministered by us, written not with ink but by the Spirit of the living God, not on tablets of stone but on tablets of flesh, that is, of the heart.

69. Followers will listen to their leader when they see his example in health, strength, vigor, vitality, and stamina.	• An example reflects what we ought to be. Leaders are being watched by God, angels, demons, and people.

Hebrews 12:1 (NIV) Therefore, since we are surrounded by such a great cloud of witnesses, let us throw off everything that hinders and the sin that so easily entangles, and let us run with perseverance the race marked out for us.

5. Leads by being an example of his message

A message fulfilled in the life of the messenger makes a leader a shining example like his Master. When there is no contradiction between the message and the messenger, both become a powerful entity for others to follow. People understand a message much better when they see it put into action.

Screaming wife beats husband in pulpit

I was attending a meeting where a preacher was sharing a message. About halfway through his message, he made a statement that his wife did not agree with. She was greatly incensed. She rose up from her seat and headed straight towards the pulpit screaming, "John, you know you are lying! You don't live that at home! Your life contradicts your message!" She was furious, lost control, and began beating him. It was an amazing episode, and amusing. He was tall and she was short.❑

The private failure of living what we preach becomes a public failure that will bring shame and degradation.

	Principle		*Comment*
70.	Every leader must sincerely aim to be the example of what God lays upon his heart to teach.	•	Living the truth makes it easy to proclaim it effectively. Truth applied is truth simplified.

Proverbs 16:23 (NKJV)   The heart of the wise teaches his mouth, and adds learning to his lips.

Principle	*Comment*

71. The leader who believes he has received truth from the Lord should live it first, enjoy it second, and share it third. It becomes life-producing in others.

- Truth lived becomes an experience that can be imparted to others. Experiences are more fruitful than concepts —they translate truth into practical reality.

Matthew 10:8 (NKJV) "Heal the sick, cleanse the lepers, raise the dead, cast out demons. Freely you have received, freely give."

---

72. As example is the most effective teacher, the leader who practices what he preaches will make it easier for his followers to obey the rules he lays down.

- To be an example one must consistently practice what he preaches, which makes it attractive for others to follow. Such a powerful life is irresistible.

Matthew 5:19 (NIV) Anyone who breaks one of the least of these commandments and teaches others to do the same will be called least in the kingdom of heaven, but whoever practices and teaches these commands will be called great in the kingdom of heaven.

Principle	*Comment*
73. A leader who endeavors to apply principles to himself before he requires them of his followers, will find a greater response because of his exemplary life.	• It is costly, but necessary, for a leader to be an example; unless he becomes an example he disqualifies himself. Seeing is more convincing than hearing.

Luke 6:42 (NKJV) "Or how can you say to your brother, 'Brother, let me remove the speck that is in your eye,' when you yourself do not see the plank that is in your own eye? Hypocrite! First remove the plank from your own eye, and then you will see clearly to remove the speck that is in your brother's eye."

| 74. A consistent leader whose words match his deeds is a walking example to his followers. | • When his words and deeds match, a leader will have no lack of followers who will cooperate with him joyfully. |

1 Samuel 3:19 (NKJV) So Samuel grew, and the LORD was with him and let none of his words fall to the ground.

Principle	*Comment*

75. Some leaders preach by precept, others by their example also, which makes them more effective.

• The influence of what we are extends far beyond what we say and do. Imbibing truth makes life a dynamic experience.

2 Corinthians 1:12 (NKJV)   For our boasting is this: the testimony of our conscience that we conducted ourselves in the world in simplicity and godly sincerity, not with fleshly wisdom but by the grace of God, and more abundantly toward you.

---

76. Exemplary leaders value discipline the most and make the utmost progress in their walk with God and in serving Him.

• Discipline transforms information into daily experience; it is the key to practical Christian living. Where there is discipline there is fulfillment.

1 Corinthians 3:19 (NKJV)   For the wisdom of this world is foolishness with God. For it is written, "He catches the wise in their own craftiness";

---

6. Leads by serving others

A leader who does not serve disqualifies himself from his role. A true leader is a true servant at heart who by his total dedication captures the hearts of his followers, who will follow him delightfully.

Traveling servant builds host a closet

I have the privilege of traveling with different brethren at different intervals, because of my calling and holding leadership seminars in every continent. On one of the trips around the world, it was indeed joyful to travel with a man of God who was talented in many ways. We would stay in the home of pastors and this man would examine the house and see what could be done to improve it—and he knew how to do it. He was well-trained and greatly talented.

I still remember the first house we stayed in. The room he and I were sleeping in had no closet. "Costa," he said, "Let's go downtown and buy some wood and build one." And that we did. He was particular to finish whatever he started. This is an attribute that greatly excites me.❏

Blessed are the people who have a servant's spirit and serve constantly without being asked. That is the Spirit of Christ, which affects people's lives the most. Some people serve once in a while when they are asked; some have to be begged to serve; some have to be coaxed, while others have to be stimulated.

He who loves richly will be generous in serving. He who serves with excellence manifests Christ in His fullness.

Principle	**Comment**

77.   The leader who expects others to serve him well, must take the lead in serving others.

• We always reap in the same proportion that we sow; this is a universal law.

Galatians 5:13 (NKJV)   For you, brethren, have been called to liberty; only do not use liberty as an opportunity for the flesh, but through love serve one another.

78.   The leader who focuses his eyes on the needs of others is moving in step with his Master, who loved and cared for people and went about doing good.

• The proof of loving is in giving to meet the needs of the destitute. Leaders must be ardent observers. They must respond quickly to every arising need.

2 Corinthians 4:5 (NKJV)   For we do not preach ourselves, but Christ Jesus the Lord, and ourselves your bondservants for Jesus' sake.

|| *Principle* | *Comment* ||

79. The ability of a leader to help his people individually, though it may be overtaxing at times, is the key to his exemplary life, beckoning them to follow in his devotion to them and to the Lord.

- The measure of our devotion determines the level of our service. When love is unlimited, sacrifice is unlimited. Love induces commitment and propels to action.

2 Corinthians 12:15 (NKJV)   And I will very gladly spend and be spent for your souls; though the more abundantly I love you, the less I am loved.

---

80. A genuine leader gives himself to his people and affects a definite change for the best in their lives.

- Laying down our lives for others affects them most. It is the proof that causes transformation.

John 15:13 (NKJV)   "Greater love has no one than this, than to lay down one's life for his friends."

Principle	**Comment**
81. A Christ-like leader, who forgets about himself and is endowed with a godly attitude toward serving others, is safe to follow.	• The more a leader loves God and gets involved in serving Him, the more he will forget about himself. Yet he will be remembered by the Lord.

John 5:30 (NKJV) "I can of Myself do nothing. As I hear, I judge; and My judgment is righteous, because I do not seek My own will but the will of the Father who sent Me."

| 82. A leader who is a load-lifter is in great demand at all seasons wherever he goes. | • When a leader is sensitized to his people's needs he shares their burdens lovingly. |

Galatians 6:2 (NKJV) Bear one another's burdens, and so fulfill the law of Christ.

---

7. Leads lovingly

A leader with a domineering spirit leads by forcing issues from the outside, while a loving leader leads by the force of his compelling love from the inside. Love stimulates the will, invigorates the desire, and solicits the full cooperation of his people. It is the Grand Master Key to the greatest accomplishments in life.

The leader who leads lovingly is followed willingly. While a leader who forces issues on people generates mounting pressures that will result in an explosive situation.

People revolt against harsh and rude president

The president of a country was known for his rebellion, arrogance, and domineering spirit. He ruled with a rod of iron. Harshness and rudeness characterized his leadership. He ruled with such a force that he demoralized his country. The morale among his own forces was eroded. Suddenly the tide turned against him. The people revolted violently and dragged him into the street to his death.❏

Mistreating people is a trait of rude character, which tends to lower people's dignity and destroy their self-esteem, rendering them ineffective. No one has the right to degrade another, either by word or by deed. People are worthy of the best treatment, which recognizes their precious value.

The end of a leader begins at the collapse of his character. He who grows up undisciplined will be spoiled all of his life, having no regard for people. Poverty of character manifests itself in mistreating others.

Principle	*Comment*

83. A kind leader who steers his operation smoothly is like a captain who steers his ship safely on a stormy sea.

• Everybody responds to the language of kindness; it is clearly understood even by the blind and the deaf.

2 Chronicles 10:6-7 (NKJV)   Then King Rehoboam consulted the elders who stood before his father Solomon while he still lived, saying, "How do you advise me to answer these people?" {7} And they spoke to him, saying, "If you are kind to these people, and please them, and speak good words to them, they will be your servants forever."

---

84. Gentle leaders are stronger in their influence than dynamite is in its destruction.

• Gentleness penetrates the spirit of man and affects a definite and remarkable change.

1 Thessalonians 2:7 (NKJV)   But we were gentle among you, just as a nursing mother cherishes her own children.

	Principle	*Comment*

85.   A sensible leader is a source of stability and strength to his people, as they behold his godly example.

- Godliness and sensibility produce a balance that leads to being a shining example.

1 Chronicles 12:17-18 (NKJV)   And David went out to meet them, and answered and said to them, "If you have come peaceably to me to help me, my heart will be united with you; but if to betray me to my enemies, since there is no wrong in my hands, may the God of our fathers look and bring judgment." {18} Then the Spirit came upon Amasai, chief of the captains, and he said: "We are yours, O David; we are on your side, O son of Jesse! Peace, peace to you, and peace to your helpers! For your God helps you." So David received them, and made them captains of the troop.

86.   Blessed is the leader who is endowed with a keen sense of justice and administers the same, for he shall be a good resemblance of his Heavenly Father.

- A justified leader must become a just leader. Many over the face of the whole world are suffering from injustice. Justice suffers the most worldwide.

Matthew 5:9 (NKJV)   Blessed are the peacemakers, For they shall be called sons of God.

Principle	Comment
87. A skillful leader never scolds his people for failing to perform, but helps them as he shows them how to develop strength where they are weak.	• Progress is built on developing people, rather than degrading them. Leaders who invest much in their people reap much. People produce their best when treated the best.

Romans 15:1 (NKJV)   We then who are strong ought to bear with the scruples of the weak, and not to please ourselves.

Principle	Comment
88. A well-mannered leader reveals his uprightness by being patient with those having bad manners. His example brings conviction to their lives.	• Endurance is an outstanding quality that modifies and beautifies a leader's manners. Endurance is stretched patience that does not snap.

John 8:7,9 (NKJV)   So when they continued asking Him, He raised Himself up and said to them, "He who is without sin among you, let him throw a stone at her first."...{9} Then those who heard it, being convicted by their conscience, went out one by one, beginning with the oldest even to the last....

Principle	*Comment*

89. The tolerance of the Lord while dealing with His people is limited by His leaders who are supposed to be the examples.

• God's dealings are for our correction and perfection. The more loving a leader is the more tolerant he is with his people.

1 Timothy 1:15-16 (NIV)   Here is a trustworthy saying that deserves full acceptance: Christ Jesus came into the world to save sinners—of whom I am the worst. {16} But for that very reason I was shown mercy so that in me, the worst of sinners, Christ Jesus might display his unlimited patience as an example for those who would believe on him and receive eternal life.

90. A strong leader is persistent and works hard on assignments, while a weak leader drives others to put everything into it, and succumb in the end.

• Thoughtfulness towards one's followers doubles their appreciation and effort. It brings their hidden best to the surface. They render their service to him joyfully.

Proverbs 21:5 (NIV)   The plans of the diligent lead to profit as surely as haste leads to poverty.

8. Chooses words carefully

Exemplary leaders choose words suitable for those who speak for the King of Kings. To them words are not cheap, but most costly and must be spoken in a manner that expresses the mind and heart of God. When we open our mouths, our words express our total personality and reveal our level of maturity, our motives, and the contents of our heart.

Advisor with the right perspective saves his head

A king called his advisors to audience. When they all arrived he had a private interview with each of them asking them the same question—"I am getting older and want to know what will happen to my children after my death." His children were reckless in their living. They were always in trouble. They mixed with the wrong crowd. They had been known to associate with dangerous gangsters and had been shot and injured several times.

Unbeknown to one another, all of the counselors, except one, said to him, "Your children are heading to an early death." The statement, repeated to him by each one, shocked him, and he ordered all of them beheaded.

When the one remaining counselor was interviewed his reply was, "Your Honor, Majesty, the King, I see you having long life that will outlive all of your children." He did not know what had happened to the other counselors. The king looked at him and was relieved and comforted by such wise words and ordered his promotion.❑

Our words can be the cause of our being beheaded or promoted. The wise choice of words and the proper approach will determine the outcome. The privilege to speak must be based on having the right thing to say in the right way.

Respectful envoy gains royal gift and promotion

A king and all his ministers were invited to a celebration of a neighboring king. Suddenly his kingdom was threatened by war that prevented them from attending. The king, as well as each minister, sent their envoys with gifts.

When they arrived, each presented the gift and gave a brief talk. They were nervous, unprepared for the occasion and mumbling their words. All of them but one displeased the king and his ministers.

The last one was given audience. He was to have been the first but had an emergency that prevented him from arriving on time. After he greeted the king with proper etiquette he commenced his very suitable words fitting to kings as the others announced for whom they were speaking. However, this representative of the king said soberly, "I speak for the King." Immediately the king and all his ministers stood up and applauded him for his choice words, his royal approach, and his respectful mannerism.

It pleased the king to send a closed note of thanks to the king who sent him. In the note he recommended him highly for promotion and praised him much for the way he spoke on behalf of his king. Most of all, he showered him with a royal gift.

When he arrived home and presented the note to his king it brought great pleasure to him and he confirmed his promotion.❏

Our words can be the cause of our being commended or reprimanded, promoted or demoted. Words are only cheap to the fool. But, to the wise they are most valuable in life. Some people who have nothing to say insist on chattering incessantly. Only those who have something to say that is meaningful and powerfully compacted with purpose know the value of words and their accountability for them after they have uttered them.

Principle	*Comment*

91. Leaders who speak the least say the most, make the least mistakes, and progress the fastest.

• When we open our mouth we are on trial. A wise leader weighs his words and expresses them carefully to the point.

Proverbs 17:27 (NKJV)   He who has knowledge spares his words, and a man of understanding is of a calm spirit.

---

92. A leader is judged by what he says and by how, when, and why he says it.

• Carefulness in speaking reveals thoughtfulness in thinking.

Psalm 19:14 (NKJV)   Let the words of my mouth and the meditation of my heart be acceptable in Your sight, O LORD, my strength and my Redeemer.

---

93. Every word a leader utters reveals the true condition of his heart and is a true revelation of who he is.

• It is better to keep the heart sanctified so that we will not suffer unnecessarily.

Luke 6:45 (NKJV)   "A good man out of the good treasure of his heart brings forth good; and an evil man out of the evil treasure of his heart brings forth evil. For out of the abundance of the heart his mouth speaks."

Principle	*Comment*
94. A successful leader is one who communicates with people in terms they can easily understand.	• The most effective leader is the one who can reach the simplest people with clarity of truth.

Galatians 3:1 (NKJV)   O foolish Galatians! Who has bewitched you that you should not obey the truth, before whose eyes Jesus Christ was clearly portrayed among you as crucified?

———————————

| 95. A leader who speaks with a skillful vocabulary will influence his hearers the more if he speaks plainly. | • Clarity of expression is more effective than complicated words, which tend to confuse and be hard to understand. |

John 16:29-30 (NKJV)   Then Jesus' disciples said, "Now you are speaking clearly and without figures of speech. {30} Now we can see that you know all things and that you do not need to have anyone ask you questions. This makes us believe that you came from God."

———————————

Principle	*Comment*
96. The leader who adopts the policy of "I will not talk about him if he is not here," unless he has a good word to say, is a good example to follow.	• If a leader does not backbite, no one will bite him back. It is safer that way for him and for others.

James 4:11 (NKJV)   Do not speak evil of one another, brethren. He who speaks evil of a brother and judges his brother, speaks evil of the law and judges the law. But if you judge the law, you are not a doer of the law but a judge.

---

97. A courteous and considerate leader who values his relationships with others, expresses himself patiently, kindly, and humbly in his dealings with them.	• An act of courtesy travels around the world and gets back to you. Courteous leaders are considerate in their approach, are sweet in their attitude, and simplify their expressions.

Ephesians 4:29 (NKJV)   Let no corrupt word proceed out of your mouth, but what is good for necessary edification, that it may impart grace to the hearers.

---

9. Is humble

Humility before God and man is a sign of a refined character. Leadership is a place of power. Power is dangerous unless humility guides it. Humility is a total realization of our nothingness, emptiness, and helplessness. It is bowing down before God on a continual basis, acknowledging His supremacy over all, His sovereignty to intervene in all, and His authority to rule over all. The leader who is not humble is bound to stumble.

True humility is born out of a revelation of the greatness of God and of the smallness of ourselves. When we see ourselves as God sees us, we realize that we are neither what we think we are, nor are we what people surmise that we are.

A revelation of God deflates our pride and keeps us safe from thinking more highly of ourselves than we ought. Neither will we be high-minded but condescend to men of low estate, taking Paul's advice in Romans 12:16. Where there is genuine humility, there is perfect safety. He who is not humble is destined to total failure due to the pride hidden in his heart. "Pride goes before destruction..." (Proverbs 16:18, nkjv)

An old friend of mine in Jerusalem left me a great legacy when he shared his thought on greatness. These were his words of wisdom before he passed away. "Costa, always remember that the greatness of a man is in his humility."

David's humble request to face Goliath

In 1 Samuel chapter 17, we have one of the most outstanding lessons on humility that King David taught us while he was still a shepherd.

His father sent him to the battlefield where for forty days and forty nights the Israelites were facing Goliath and his army. When David heard the words of Goliath defying the armies of the living God, he was greatly incensed. David made it clear that he was willing to accept the challenge and face Goliath.

When he was called before the king, verse 32 to verse 36, David tried to prove his willingness, readiness, and ability to face Goliath (since he had past experiences in facing a lion and a bear, ripping them apart because God's power was with him).

He was endeavoring to show the king that the Lord, who was with him there, would be with him when he faced Goliath. Three times in these verses he addresses the king as "your servant," "your servant," "your servant."

A humble spirit such as this will be guaranteed a promotion from God. The Bible says, "Humble yourselves under the mighty hand of God, that He may [promote] you in due time" (1 Peter 5:6, nkjv); and David was promoted.❑

It is said that a humble man never blows his own horn in public. Humility is a precious quality that makes us feel smaller as we grow greater. God is searching for great men to be small enough to allow God to use them mightily. The humble has the full support of God in whatever he does. This is the reason he prospers on the way.

Humility is always in season and is accepted by every culture worldwide. Humble people are greatly admired yet they touch more lives than powerful people who are greatly feared only. True greatness is not found in bulging muscles but in humility of spirit that serves without a thought of recompense.

Principle	*Comment*

98. An exemplary leader will be the first to die to his ego and drop his logical defense, willing to lose an argument and gain the friendship of his subordinates, as he endeavors to solve an arising problem.

• Leaders who have died to themselves have no need for unnecessary arguments to defend their egos. Guarding the dignity of others is a solemn obligation of leaders—especially to their faithful followers.

1 Corinthians 13:5 (NKJV)   [Love] does not behave rudely, does not seek its own, is not provoked, thinks no evil;

---

99. The leader who continually lives with a spirit of humility and is quick to repent when he does wrong, becomes an example for others to follow.

• The quicker we repent, the easier it is for us. The longer we delay repentance the harder it becomes. Why live with bitter regrets?

1 John 1:9 (NIV)   If we confess our sins, he is faithful and just and will forgive us our sins and purify us from all unrighteousness.

Principle	*Comment*
100. When a leader is quick to apologize and honestly takes the blame when he recognizes his mistake —instead of defending it —he grows taller in the eyes of his followers and teaches them an exemplary lesson in humility.	• He who covers up his mistake is wrong, but he who defends it is doubly wrong. All arguments to prove we are right when we are wrong are futile. Arguments never solve problems, but they tend to complicate them and turn them into crises.

2 Samuel 12:13 (NKJV)   So David said to Nathan, "I have sinned against the LORD." And Nathan said to David, "The LORD also has put away your sin; you shall not die."

10. Is receptive to those the Lord has given him

No leader is sufficient apart from the contributions of his colleagues, especially the input of his own people.

Employee suggestions make company #1

The president of one of the most successful airlines published an article in their monthly magazine offered free to their passengers. It drew my attention and won my admiration and respect.

He saw the need for the input of all his employees and announced a financial compensation to any valuable suggestion that would contribute to the progress of the company. His exhortation found a favorable reaction that made his airline #1, due to his receptivity, respectful consideration, and wise evaluation of the suggestions offered.❑

Principle	*Comment*
101. When a leader is receptive to wise counsel, it helps refine his character and will promote him in the ranks of exemplary leadership.	• Wise counsel enriches a leader's character and makes him a shining example, if he is humble and receptive. The measure of our receptivity determines our progress.

Proverbs 12:1 (NKJV)   Whoever loves instruction loves knowledge, but he who hates correction is stupid.

Principle	*Comment*
102. A wise leader establishes rapport with his followers keeping the lines of communication open.	• Communication is the lifeline of relationships. Much in life depends on how we communicate.

1 Peter 5:5 (NKJV)   Likewise you younger people, submit yourselves to your elders. Yes, all of you be submissive to one another, and be clothed with humility, for "God resists the proud, But gives grace to the humble."

---

103. The leader who makes himself visible, accessible, and open to his people, will have a smooth operation all the way.	• The availability of a leader relaxes the operation and prevents tension and contention. A leader who is at rest in God accomplishes the most.

Acts 20:17-20 (NIV)   From Miletus, Paul sent to Ephesus for the elders of the church. {18} When they arrived, he said to them: "You know how I lived the whole time I was with you, from the first day I came into the province of Asia. {19} I served the Lord with great humility and with tears, although I was severely tested by the plots of the Jews. {20} You know that I have not hesitated to preach anything that would be helpful to you but have taught you publicly and from house to house."

Principle	**Comment**
104. A caring leader must realize that he is being watched by others and needs to heed their comments, protests, and commendations, if he is to improve in his leadership.	• Leaders who take heed to the input of others benefit the most. They are enriched and become resourceful. They are wise for being receptive and considerate.

2 Chronicles 10:15-19 (NKJV)   So the king [Rehoboam] did not listen to the people;...{16}Now when all Israel saw that the king did not listen to them, the people answered the king, saying: "What share have we in David? We have no inheritance in the son of Jesse. Every man to your tents, O Israel! Now see to your own house, O David!" So all Israel departed to their tents...{19}So Israel has been in rebellion against the house of David to this day.

---

105. A wise leader never manipulates or forces issues, but resorts to a dialogue policy to satisfy all concerned.	• Leaders who are good negotiators are the most successful. Wise negotiation satisfies everyone.

2 Timothy 2:24 (NKJV)   And a servant of the Lord must not quarrel but be gentle to all, able to teach, patient,

C. In relationship to HIMSELF

A leader who is at peace with God and secure in himself, will be at peace with others. He believes the truth, lives the truth, and speaks the truth. His disciplined life exhibits commendable qualities that endear him to his followers. He has been proved and approved in character and performance. He has been anointed and appointed by God to carry on his calling against all odds, be they unjustified accusations, misjudgments of his motives, or misinterpretations of his actions. He is consistent in his walk with God. He does not live for the pleasure of the moment, but everything he thinks, says, and does contributes to his eternal goal.

He is a man of principle, not of convenience, and he knows the value of time and how to invest it in eternity. He guards himself from the blind spots of life and moves swiftly toward accomplishing God's will as his top priority in life. He guards against all detours that hinder others in their heavenly pursuit, and takes his accountability to God and man most seriously.

Leader overcomes jealous criticism and excels
A leader was shredded by the unmerciful criticism of some of his colleagues as they jealously beheld God's blessings upon his life and ministry. He refused to allow the episode to lessen his zeal, or dampen his spirit and discourage him in his pursuit of excellence. He moved forward unscathed, realizing that criticism can either make him bitter or better. He chose the better and excelled through it.❏

No one can whitewash himself by blackening another. People who butcher others by their sharp tongue, will one day cut their own throat. Jealousy corrodes from within and leaves its victim naked of all commendable virtues. A leader who maintains a right spirit is able to control his actions as well as his reactions, even in the face of the most destructive provocations.

1. Has integrity

A leader's integrity protects him from the onslaughts of the enemy and the viciousness of his oppressors. He is firm in his convictions and sound in his doctrine. He is incorruptible because of his strong adherence to divine principles. His truthfulness and uprightness add luster to his personality. He can be trusted by God and man.

Integrity is the backbone of character. It is the jewel that makes a leader sparkle in the midst of gross darkness.

Cordial leader's integrity withstands attack

A leader, who comes from a country where the culture and the prevailing custom is for people to hug each other and kiss each other on both cheeks as a greeting, traveled to another country where people are stiff and rigid in their mannerisms.

He was not fully aware of their customs and continued greeting people the way he grew up. One lady accused him to her pastor of having wrong motives. They began to spread rumors against this leader. He did not retaliate or react negatively when he became aware of what had happened. He did not have to defend himself. His integrity proved itself to all who knew him.

However, from that day on the leader did take precautions and only shook hands with people. To his surprise many of them would ask, "Where are my hug and kisses?"❑

Affectionate people display their emotions openly without reservations. Quality of character cannot be tarnished regardless of how many lives it touches. It is the same with a character that is noted for its integrity.

It is a well known fact that a thief who is guilty of stealing thinks everybody is a thief. It is impossible to live a life that will live up to everyone's expectations.

Principle	*Comment*
106. The leader who is a man of integrity gains the favor of God and man. His transparency reveals his depth in God.	• Integrity is the root; transparency is the fruit. When a leader is pure in heart he hides nothing. He revels in walking in the light.

1 John 1:7 (NKJV) But if we walk in the light as He is in the light, we have fellowship with one another, and the blood of Jesus Christ His Son cleanses us from all sin.

| 107. What a leader really is determines what he does, for the inner quality of his character will become evident to all. | • Nothing is hidden that shall not be revealed, regardless of all human efforts to cover up. Transparency is highly commendable. |

Matthew 12:35 (NKJV) "A good man out of the good treasure of his heart brings forth good things, and an evil man out of the evil treasure brings forth evil things."

Principle	*Comment*
108. Regardless of how talented, intelligent, or experienced a leader may be, what impresses his people most is who he is in his daily life.	• The stability of his character stands out most; it speaks the loudest and shines the farthest. He exhibits a wholesome relationship with his people.

Acts 11:23-24 (NKJV)   When he [Barnabas] came and had seen the grace of God, he was glad, and encouraged them all that with purpose of heart they should continue with the Lord. {24} For he was a good man, full of the Holy Spirit and of faith. And a great many people were added to the Lord.

———————

109. Give a person a position of leadership, at any level, and you will soon see things about him that you've never seen before.	• A position unveils both hidden virtues and hidden vices. The undue pressures of life test the core of our character.

1 Timothy 3:6,10 (NKJV)   not a novice, lest being puffed up with pride he fall into the same condemnation as the devil. {10} But let these also first be tested; then let them serve as deacons, being found blameless.

———————

2. Has developed good character traits

Character is the sum total of a leader's characteristics. Such characteristics affect his spirit, motives, attitudes, thinking, speaking, and all his activities relating to God, to people, and to himself. A leader must live with mature attributes so that when people get to know him, they will get to know Christ better.

Stifled teacher reaps a great harvest

A teacher, reading an article from a far country, realized a need in that country for the subjects that were her specialty. She applied for the position and was accepted. She had always wanted to be a witness for the Lord in her profession.

The first day she arrived, she met the principal who told her that her qualifications are acceptable and they would like to have a contract for two years. When she began to fill out the contract the principal said, "Before you sign the contract, I would like to ask you a private question." She replied, "Yes." He asked, "What is your religion?" She said, "I am a born again Christian." He said, "We are not Christians here and we want to ask you not to mention anything about Christ as long as you are a teacher in this school." She said to him, "Thank you for letting me know your requirements. However, I will not sign the contract and I will leave today for home." He was shocked. But she was determined that she could not teach there. He begged her to go to the hotel that night, meditate on his request and come back the next morning with her answer.

She did as he had asked. She spent most of the night praying, and asking the Lord to speak to her heart. She was brokenhearted, weeping, "Lord, I spent much money to come here with the intent of witnessing to Your saving grace. Now, I cannot do it."

The Lord said to her, "In your country you talked about Me. Here, in this country, let your life be lived in such a way that My life will shine through you. It costs less to preach the gospel than to live the gospel. Remember, I came to serve, not to be served. Be a servant to these people."

She went back to the principal the next morning, signed the contract, and agreed to say nothing. As she was praying, God led her to volunteer tutoring the worst students in the school. She began to minister to them one by one. They were noted for being lazy, disruptive, vulgar, and they had no initiative. However, through her loving ministry, little by little, the worst of them became the best in the school. Her fame spread to the families of all the students.

She could hardly cope with the amount of invitations to visit the homes of students and tutor them. At the end of her two year contract she was greatly appreciated, loved, and accepted in their culture.

On the last day of school, she met with the principal. She thanked him for the opportunity of being with them and asked for her passport to be returned as she was leaving the following day. He refused to give her the passport. He said that the parents of the students had a special meeting. They called him to advise him never to give this teacher her passport back, even though this was the custom after the contract expired. But in her case, she should stay as long as she lives, because she had proven to be a loving person who had served these people untiringly.

She said to him, "I will promise to come back. However, I must at least visit my family for a period of three to six months." When she promised to return he agreed to return her passport. She realized that God had given her grace in His sight and in the sight of the people.

She then dared to ask the principal, "Since this is my last day in school, would you permit me to talk about my Jesus?" "Oh!" he said, "You may talk about Him all day today."

He never realized the impact that one day could make on the students. He did not know the power of the Holy Spirit. She was so excited. She went to her apartment, exchanged the textbooks for the Bible, and came back rejoicing in the Lord.

All day she would travel from Genesis to Revelation in the Bible, preaching without any restrictions. At the end of the day she asked the students in the school, "Now you have heard all about my Jesus. How many of you would like to be like Him and accept Him as your Savior?"

Many of their hands went up. Sitting before her, in the first row, were the worst students that she had helped. They became top in their class. One of them was especially unbearable. He terrified all the students. She expected this one and the rest of his gang to raise their hands. None of them responded as they were following his move. But there were tears coming down his face. She asked him, "Don't you want to become like Jesus?" "No, I don't know who Jesus is. But all the time I have wanted to be like you." "Oh!" she said, "I am like Jesus." He said, "If you are like Jesus, then I want to be like Jesus." He and his gang accepted Christ as their personal Savior. There was much joy at the end of that day.❏

Living the gospel, demonstrating a loving service by helping others, is the greatest proof of the life of Christ. This draws people to Him. The world needs more people who will walk with God, than those who only talk about God.

Wholehearted service that knows no limit to its sacrifice, exemplifies the very life of Christ, who said, "I am among you as one who serves." (Luke 22:27, niv) True service to others is the badge of the practical Christian life that glorifies the Lord.

Principle	*Comment*
110. An exemplary leader is an inspiration to unmotivated people who draw their inspiration from the quality of his life and character, and arise to follow him.	• For a leader to be a proper example he must be dead to himself and live purely for God, proving it by serving his people sacrificially. He regards the welfare of his people as top priority.

2 Timothy 2:10-11 (NKJV)   Therefore I endure all things for the sake of the elect, that they also may obtain the salvation which is in Christ Jesus with eternal glory. {11} This is a faithful saying: for if we died with Him, we shall also live with Him.

---

111. A good reputation is a leader's best asset.	• Reputation is the reflection of one's character.

3 John 1:11-12 (KJV)   Beloved, follow not that which is evil, but that which is good. He that doeth good is of God: but he that doeth evil hath not seen God. {12} Demetrius hath good report of all men, and of the truth itself: yea, and we also bear record; and ye know that our record is true.

Principle	*Comment*

112. A leader who has gained a good name by his wholesome behavior, will discover it keeps its luster in the dark.

- A well-developed character behaves the same in testing as well as in relaxed times, all due to being deeply rooted in God.

Proverbs 22:1 (NKJV) A good name is to be chosen rather than great riches, loving favor rather than silver and gold.

———————————

113. A cautious leader endeavors to be watchful, because he realizes that the impressions he makes on others and the expressions he displays, reveal his inner motives and attitudes and the spirit behind them.

- To be our best for God requires our utmost carefulness. Leaders who are alert and watchful prove themselves the best in the arena of life. More people pray than watch—and wonder why they fail —when the Bible says watch and pray.

Proverbs 15:28 (NKJV) The heart of the righteous studies how to answer, but the mouth of the wicked pours forth evil.

———————————

Principle	*Comment*
114. It is expected of every leader to make his health fitness a top priority, if he is to become an example to his people and be able to perform with the efficiency his position demands.	• No unhealthy leader can be his best for God. Only when we are in the best of health can we be our best for God. Adhering to the principles of nutrition, coupled with discipline, is a daily must.

3 John 1:2 (NKJV)   Beloved, I pray that you may prosper in all things and be in health, just as your soul prospers.

| 115. The leader who is prompt not only shows respect for himself, but also gains the confidence of others. | • It takes consistent discipline to always be on time. Inconsistency infringes on the time of others. |

2 Samuel 20:4-5 (NKJV)   And the king said to Amasa, "Assemble the men of Judah for me within three days, and be present here yourself." {5} So Amasa went to assemble the men of Judah. But he delayed longer than the set time which David had appointed him.

Principle	*Comment*
116. A leader who is in tune with God is always on time in performing His will, for he moves according to God's timetable.	• Divine intimacy results in divine accuracy, revealing a depth of love and dedication. A leader who is in harmony with God moves in step with Him.

Ecclesiastes 8:5 (NKJV)   He who keeps his command will experience nothing harmful; And a wise man's heart discerns both time and judgment,

---

117. Exemplary leaders set the ground rules by their behavior more than by their words.	• What we are speaks louder than what we say (even with a microphone).

1 Timothy 4:12 (NKJV)   Let no one despise your youth, but be an example to the believers in word, in conduct, in love, in spirit, in faith, in purity.

---

3. Lives the truth

A leader who believes the truth and lives the truth is heard when he speaks. Truth obeyed produces a leader that exemplifies the qualities of Christ. It liberates him from all bondages that hinder his development into maturity. Truth lived fortifies a leader and helps him face all life's crises with confidence.

There is no greatness when truth is ignored. Truth fulfilled in a life produces boldness and makes a leader's face like flint in the face of all contrariness of life. There is no retreat in the life of a leader who is impregnated with the truth. Paul exhorts, "Let the word of Christ dwell in you richly in all wisdom." (Colossians 3:16, nkjv)

Speaking the truth cost John the Baptist his head
Though living the truth is costly, in some instances speaking the truth can be more costly. John the Baptist confronted Herod that it was unlawful for him to take his brother's wife, and Herodias hated him for telling him the truth. (Matthew 14:1-16). When the occasion presented itself, Herod took revenge and ordered John the Baptist to be beheaded. Speaking the truth cost John the Baptist his life.❏

He that compromises his principles and settled convictions cannot live with himself. Honest people would rather sacrifice themselves than sacrifice their principles. Compromisers are losers at large. They lose self-respect and the respect of others, and they are ostracized in a society that maintains high standards.

Principle	*Comment*
118. The leader who imbibes truth and conforms to it is qualified to lead others into the same realm. What a blessing he becomes.	• Personified truth is most powerful—it is proved by an experienced leader who became resourceful to his people.

James 1:21 (NKJV) Therefore lay aside all filthiness and overflow of wickedness, and receive with meekness the implanted word, which is able to save your souls.

| 119. A leader must be a fulfiller of truth at all times, to be an example worthy to be followed. | • Exemplary leaders are a mighty force; their lives exemplify Christ in all His graciousness and might. |

1 Thessalonians 1:6-7 (NKJV) And you became followers of us and of the Lord, having received the word in much affliction, with joy of the Holy Spirit, {7} so that you became examples to all in Macedonia and Achaia who believe.

Principle	*Comment*

120. Truth must become life to a leader in his daily experience before it can become life to his people.

- When truth is enjoyed and lived by a leader, it ministers the same to his people. Truth exercised becomes real experientially.

John 6:63 (NKJV)   "It is the Spirit who gives life; the flesh profits nothing. The words that I speak to you are spirit, and they are life.

---

121. The leader who lives the truth, before he shares it, has a powerful effect when he opens his mouth.

- Eloquent living supersedes eloquent preaching. Speaking out of experience produces a rich impartation.

Acts 1:1 (NIV)   In my former book, Theophilus, I wrote about all that Jesus began to do and to teach

---

122. Truth becomes more powerful when it is lived out in a leader's life. Such leaders influence others to follow their godly example.

- Truth lived out reveals the living God. People become enamored by such a clear revelation, which causes them to draw near to Him.

Luke 9:57 (NKJV)   Now it happened as they journeyed on the road, that someone said to Him, "Lord, I will follow You wherever You go."

---

4. Lives with eternity in view

Whatever a leader thinks, says, and does, must have eternal significance. He values time, talents, giftings, and substance, and uses them wisely to contribute to eternal dividends. He who thinks of time, lives for time; but whoever is obsessed with eternity, lives for eternity.

He who lives on earth with eternity in view, lives all of his life to invest in eternity. He guards himself against wasting his time, talents, gifting, abilities, money, or relationships. He lives responsibly, for he knows the seriousness of his accountability to God and to man.

Ruler inquires about eternal life

There is a story about a ruler who came to ask Christ a vitally important question, which is being asked by millions in every generation. "Good Master, what shall I do to inherit eternal life?" (Luke 18:18-24, kjv)

This ruler was highly educated. He had a high position, name, fame, popularity, and great riches. He had all the pleasures of life at his fingertip. Yet, deep inside, he was dissatisfied, disappointed, and disillusioned. He knew life could be better than it was. He knew life was eternal.

Christ's answer to him was, "Sell everything you have and give to the poor, and you shall have treasure in heaven." (vs. 22, niv) Christ was saying to him, "since your desire is to go to heaven, convert all your assets to heavenly currency." Jesus came to preach the gospel to the poor.

The word "poor" does not only mean to be without money. It means to be without God. A person can be a multi-billionaire, but if Christ has not become his personal savior, and God has not become his father, he is poor. Christ came to enrich us with the presence of God, which money cannot buy.

Giving of your time and your money to reach the poor who are without God is the heart of the gospel. The gospel is God's message of enrichment to poverty-stricken people who are separated from God because of sin.

The rich ruler did not pay careful attention to the answer to his question. It is better to die poor while investing your money in reaching people who are without the gospel, than to die rich, hoarding your money, and depriving those who have not heard the good news.

The ruler wanted something for nothing. He wanted the pleasures of this life and eternity at the same time. It is unwise to work hard to accumulate wealth, and then to leave your money here and have no rewards in eternity.❏

Principle	*Comment*
123. The leader of the hour is the one who makes every hour count for eternity.	• Time is a borrowed trust from eternity and must be used to fulfill God's eternal purpose.

Ephesians 5:15-16 (NKJV) See then that you walk circumspectly, not as fools but as wise, {16} redeeming the time, because the days are evil.

Principle	*Comment*
124. When a leader values eternity of great importance and invests his life, time, talents, gifts, and substance in it, he begins to live a life that's worth following.	• Leaders who live for eternity will not be attracted to things in the world or lured by its vain offers. They are steadfast in their walk with God and settled in their convictions.

2 Peter 3:10-14 (NKJV)   But the day of the Lord will come as a thief in the night, in which the heavens will pass away with a great noise, and the elements will melt with fervent heat; both the earth and the works that are in it will be burned up. {11} Therefore, since all these things will be dissolved, what manner of persons ought you to be in holy conduct and godliness, {12}...? {13}...{14}...be diligent to be found by Him in peace, without spot and blameless;

5. Is disciplined

Discipline is the key to growth and productivity. It must be systematic to consistently accomplish its goal. Discipline is the Master Key to the development of character, which helps leaders with their behavior as they relate to people. If we discipline ourselves, no one else has to discipline us and we make life easier for ourselves and for others, even for God.

To be disciplined is having the ability to obey instructions willingly. Knowledge is a servant to experience when discipline is put into action. The best knowledge, instruction, and revelation is useless without the discipline to use it. It does not matter whether it is in a person's personal life, home life, or public life.

Two frivolous military group leaders shot

A king appointed a qualified and proven strategist to train his leaders. The strategist separated them into two groups. He chose two of the kings choicest and closest friends and invested much time to prepare them for their new role as instructors for the two groups of leaders.

The time came for his first round of inspections. He lined up the two groups with their two leaders standing in front and gave the command to move to the right in a quick march. No one responded. The two leaders where giggling and laughing, which distracted the rest. Then the commander gave the same command, except to turn to the left. The same thing happened, no one responded. The distracted leaders did not pay attention to the seriousness of the chief commander's instructions.

The chief commander ordered the two training leaders to be shot immediately. When the order was carried out, he then gave the command to both groups and they promptly obeyed. They passed the test of self-discipline to obey.

We only obey to the measure that we discipline ourselves. We discipline ourselves to develop character, expertise, or cooperation with others to accomplish a common goal.

When the king heard what had happened, he asked his chief commander the reason for his quick action. His reply was, "In military rules we take discipline seriously. Orders must be obeyed promptly. If not, instant judgment awakens others to the seriousness of obeying the commander." The king acquiesced.❏

Character reaches the height of its maturity through self-discipline. He who learns self-discipline early in life will succeed all of his life. He who wants the best for himself will continue to discipline himself and will welcome the discipline of others, if needed, knowing it is for his best interest.

Principle	*Comment*
125. The most effective leader follows the example of Christ by emptying himself of all that plagues humanity: love of money; pride, popularity, name, and fame; a desire to rule with a rod of iron; to manipulate, connive, and beguile; etc., etc., etc.	• Jesus emptied Himself to reveal the Father; we can only reveal Christ by denouncing all that is contrary to Him. Yielding to the Holy Spirit allows Him to excavate us completely and bring forth the likeness of Christ in fullness.

Philippians 2:6-8 (NKJV)   who, being in the form of God, did not consider it robbery to be equal with God, {7} but made Himself of no reputation, taking the form of a bondservant, and coming in the likeness of men. {8} And being found in appearance as a man, He humbled Himself and became obedient to the point of death, even the death of the cross.

Principle	**Comment**
126. Real discipline is systematic—not sporadic or occasional. Realistic leaders know that truth practically, and they apply the rule strictly to themselves.	• Discipline shapes our character and gives us favor with God and man. The disciplined leader lives with a healthy self-image.

1 Corinthians 9:27 (NKJV)   But I discipline my body and bring it into subjection, lest, when I have preached to others, I myself should become disqualified.

---

127. To be an example, a leader must exert extra effort in consistent discipline in his life, because others look up to him for the extra qualities they have seen in him.	• Living 100% for God supersedes all the extras of life. Love is either 100% or it is not love at all. Wholehearted commitment brings security and fulfillment to love.

Titus 2:7-8 (NKJV)   in all things showing yourself to be a pattern of good works; in doctrine showing integrity, reverence, incorruptibility, {8} sound speech that cannot be condemned, that one who is an opponent may be ashamed, having nothing evil to say of you.

Principle	*Comment*
128. An undisciplined leader has no right to lead, for he is not an example of what his followers ought to be.	• When a person becomes an example, he then has the right to lead. He who is undisciplined has no place in leadership.

Hebrews 6:12 (KJV)   That ye be not slothful, but followers of them who through faith and patience inherit the promises.

---

129. A leader who has mastered the art of concentration accomplishes the most in every operation and project he undertakes.	• Concentration, which is the discipline of the mind, is a key to every worthwhile accomplishment.

Isaiah 50:7 (NKJV)   "For the Lord GOD will help Me; therefore I will not be disgraced; therefore I have set My face like a flint, and I know that I will not be ashamed."

Principle	*Comment*

130. The strength of a leader lies in the measure he is able to control himself and master his desires with a determined attitude to exemplify Christ.

- There can be no exemplary living without consistent discipline. No one will follow an inconsistent and unsteady leader whose discipline is sporadic.

2 Timothy 2:20-21 (NKJV)   But in a great house there are not only vessels of gold and silver, but also of wood and clay, some for honor and some for dishonor. {21} Therefore if anyone cleanses himself from the latter, he will be a vessel for honor, sanctified and useful for the Master, prepared for every good work.

---

131. The leader who refuses correction when he needs it forfeits his perfection.

- Correction is the way to perfection; no one is above correction, except God.

Proverbs 15:10 (NKJV)   Harsh discipline is for him who forsakes the way, and he who hates correction will die.

Principle	*Comment*

132. People find it easy to submit to the discipline of a disciplined leader because of his godly example.

• The measure of self-discipline makes the difference among leaders. The more disciplined one is, the more effective he becomes.

2 Timothy 1:7 (NIV)   For God did not give us a spirit of timidity, but a spirit of power, of love and of self-discipline.

---

133. While an undisciplined leader attempts to force discipline on his subordinates, a disciplined leader affects them by his example.

• A disciplined leader motivates his people by his mannerisms and diligence. Influence supersedes forced discipline.

2 Thessalonians 3:6-9 (NIV)   In the name of the Lord Jesus Christ, we command you, brothers, to keep away from every brother who is idle and does not live according to the teaching you received from us. {7} For you yourselves know how you ought to follow our example. We were not idle when we were with you, {8}...{9} We did this,...to make ourselves a model for you to follow.

---

6. Is consistent in private and public life

Right relationship with God based on a leader's submission to His revealed will, gives his life inner stability. It helps make him genuine and transparent before God and man. He who lives a double life suffers from inner defeat, but he who lives consistently at home with a perfect heart (home is our boot camp) is able to live outside his home victoriously.

A leader's relationship with God is solidified through submission, which fortifies him to face all temptations with firmness and assures the victory. Wholehearted submission to God deepens a leader's roots in God. The deeper the roots are the more abundant the fruit will be.

Business leader's reputation sparks his acquittal

A leader of a large business, who had gained the respect of the community and the cooperation of his followers, faced a situation that was causing him considerable concern. His subordinate, who was second in command, instigated a scandal that affected many responsible people in the company. When the investigations took their course, everyone in his family was questioned about him.

His wife gave excellent testimony of his consistency in living a godly, Christian life. His sons, ages 10 years to 25 years, spoke highly of their father's loving and kind treatment, and of the joy he brings to the entire family. His neighbors could not find enough good words to describe the quality of his character, the way he related to them, his interests in their welfare, and his help.

Most of his workers spoke highly of him and never doubted his fairness. In fact they reveled in his leadership. When the investigations were over, he was acquitted of all suspicion and gained a greater respect in the community.❑

Honesty and submission lead to consistency. However, having wickedness, hypocrisy, and a double standard in our life brings shame. Shame is unfitting for a leader.

Principle	*Comment*
134. A mature leader manifests Christ consistently both in private and in public.	• His depth of relationship with Christ is the secret of manifesting Him to his followers.

2 Corinthians 4:10-11 (NKJV)   always carrying about in the body the dying of the Lord Jesus, that the life of Jesus also may be manifested in our body. {11} For we who live are always delivered to death for Jesus' sake, that the life of Jesus also may be manifested in our mortal flesh.

---

135. The private life of a leader, whether he is godly or ungodly, has a bearing on his followers.	• We influence people both consciously and unconsciously. Influence has a penetrating effect that transforms lives.

1 Timothy 5:24-25 (NKJV)   Some men's sins are clearly evident, preceding them to judgment, but those of some men follow later. {25} Likewise, the good works of some are clearly evident, and those that are otherwise cannot be hidden.

Principle	**Comment**
136. The strongest testimony of a leader comes from his own family.	• That is his real testimony; it counts the most. How he is viewed at home is extremely important.

1 Timothy 3:5 (NKJV)   (for if a man does not know how to rule his own house, how will he take care of the church of God?);

---

137. How a leader behaves at home reveals his true person whatever his level of maturity.	• A leader's home is his testing ground; the way he loves and treats his family is most important.

Ephesians 5:25 (NKJV)   Husbands, love your wives, just as Christ also loved the church and gave Himself for her,

---

138. Determined leaders transmit a great measure of their effectiveness to others by their consistency and persistency.	• Without consistency of character there will be no persistency in performance. Such attributes are not optional, but a divine requirement.

1 Corinthians 15:58 (NKJV)   Therefore, my beloved brethren, be steadfast, immovable, always abounding in the work of the Lord, knowing that your labor is not in vain in the Lord.

---

7. Is secure and at peace where the Lord has placed him

A leader who is totally submitted to God and fully recon-ciled to His will, lives securely and has peace and tranquillity, regardless of the adverse circumstances he may face. When the peace of God rules in the heart of a leader, he will continue to find clear direction for his path.

Right relationship with God brings security and solidity. This will firm up a person's standing and help him in all circumstances. When we are secure in God we cannot be threatened, we will not vacillate in our walk with Him, we are immune from compro-mising His principles and are strong in our convictions.

A secure leader will take steady steps toward fulfilling the will of God. Nothing will daunt him. The contrariness of life will not deter him. He moves like a divine bulldozer toward his God-given goal. People will follow a secure leader and give him all their cooperation while having complete rest in their spirit.

Leaders of all levels are certain to face all types of misunder-standings, accusations, criticisms, and attacks on their character and performance. Leaders will experience discontentment in their administration, slander, persecution, turmoil from within as well as without, and at times failures. All these things are a part of the price a leader pays to be in the forefront, leading the way.

King David stays on course through confidence in God

King David was a man known for being anchored in God. He, too, went through numerous adversities in the course of his life. These adversities seemed to be characterized by battles from within and without. Studying his life is one of the greatest chal-lenges to any leader who really wants to have super quality in his virtues, excellence in his administration, and freedom in his performance. He had a secret that he passes to all his leaders. He states, "My heart is fixed, O God, my heart is fixed: I will sing and give praise." (Psalm 57:7, kjv)

Ships always face the possibilities of high seas and tempestuous waves that can destroy them. A good ship will always have a good anchor. This will determine its stability in the course of its journey through the tempests of life.

David's heart was anchored and settled in God. He had a revelation of God's greatness. He exclaimed, "Great is the Lord, and greatly to be praised." (Psalm 48:1) Many leaders of all levels come on the scene only to succumb when the contrariness of life rises against them. They don't have settled confidence in God.❏

Principle	*Comment*
139. The leader who does not vie for high position or greater recognition usually accomplishes more, for credit from men means little to him.	• Leaders are at their best when they do all things as unto the Lord. It is far better to be approved by God than to have the applause of men.

Colossians 3:23-24 (NKJV) And whatever you do, do it heartily, as to the Lord and not to men, knowing that from the Lord you will receive the reward of the inheritance; for you serve the Lord Christ.

Principle	*Comment*
140. An exemplary leader is more concerned with his being in the right place with the right spirit than with setting others in their right place.	• When we move with divine accuracy we exemplify Christ. Fulfillment in life is the result of being led by the Holy Spirit.

1 Timothy 4:16 (NKJV) Take heed to yourself and to the doctrine. Continue in them, for in doing this you will save both yourself and those who hear you.

| 141. Great leaders are great because they recognize their smallness before God. | • A revelation of the greatness of God shows us how small we really are and humbles us before Him. |

Micah 6:8 (NIV) He has showed you, O man, what is good. And what does the LORD require of you? To act justly and to love mercy and to walk humbly with your God.

Principle	*Comment*

142. A secure and honest leader is not afraid to share the weaknesses and failures that God has helped him to overcome, to help his people and encourage them along the way.

- We are what we are by the grace of God. We owe it to Him to acknowledge His goodness through praise and by sharing it with others.

2 Corinthians 12:9 (NKJV)   And He said to me, "My grace is sufficient for you, for My strength is made perfect in weakness." Therefore most gladly I will rather boast in my infirmities, that the power of Christ may rest upon me.

---

143. A leader's attitude toward his own weaknesses and failures is reflected in his reactions to the failures of others.

- If a leader lives under condemnation he becomes condemnatory; if he lives with progressive liberation, he becomes liberating.

Galatians 6:1 (NKJV)   Brethren, if a man is overtaken in any trespass, you who are spiritual restore such a one in a spirit of gentleness, considering yourself lest you also be tempted.

Principle	*Comment*
144. A peaceful leader endeavors to follow peace with all men and prevails, even under severe, strenuous, and explosive circumstances. In so doing, he exemplifies the life of Christ.	• Inner calmness results in outer quietness. Leaders who have peace with God enjoy the peace of God in their lives. The deeper the roots the more abundant the fruit in all seasons.

Romans 14:19 (NKJV)   Therefore let us pursue the things which make for peace and the things by which one may edify another.

---

145. A leader can lead peacefully in the midst of raging battles when he is at peace with God and moves with Him with a clear conscience.	• After a leader receives peace from God, his enjoyment of it is dependent upon his maintaining it through prompt obedience.

John 16:33 (NIV)   "I have told you these things, so that in me you may have peace. In this world you will have trouble. But take heart! I have overcome the world."

III. The DEVELOPMENT PROCESS

A. DEVELOPMENT into an Exemplary Leader

Every stage of development in life requires vision, short and long range goals, and constant discipline, coupled with determination supported by a persistent faith. The desire to "become" is essential to initiative. We only become what we desire to be. The rate of development depends on each individual's pace, whether he is slow, moderate, or fast in the pursuit of his ultimate purpose. Development into an exemplary leader requires the highest price in discipline and accuracy in every area of life and performance. Millions worldwide are searching for exemplary leaders to follow and emulate, hoping for a better life, better living, and more harmonious relationships, which are necessary for full cooperation in accomplishing great feats.

Seeing affects people much more than hearing or reading. Exemplary leaders can meet the needs of all, especially the underprivileged who cannot read or write. Exemplary leaders stand out among all types and levels of leadership. Their lives are crystal clear shining as the sun at noonday. The need for such leaders hinders the development of many worldwide.

Those who aspire to become exemplary leaders must take their role seriously. They must live and perform in the public eye, allowing scrutiny of their lives, which provides safety for the people.

Each step a leader takes toward becoming an example is more costly than the previous one. He must reach the deepest realms of dedication and commitment—even at the cost of his own life.

African evangelist braves the perils of the jungle

An African evangelist, related the story of his ministry by saying that he lived in a remote tribe that was adjacent to a hostile tribe. As he would go from village to village, he would have to pass through the thick jungle that surrounded them, endangering his life and being threatened by the other tribe. Each time he left home he would say good-bye to his family, for it could be the last time he would see them because of the dangers in the jungle.

He said he learned to be a fast runner—every time he was attacked by lions and other wild animals. He became skillful in climbing trees—faster than the cats. He also mastered the skill of jumping from tree to tree, when fiercely attacked by a fast aggressor. The only animal he abhorred was the elephant —no matter which tree he climbed the elephant pulled it down.❏

Such an exemplary leader is a picture of someone who is dead to himself and alive unto God; he could say with another reckless pioneer of the Faith, "I die daily." Some who pursue this path give up when fiery trials and temptation assail them to reveal their caliber and refine their character.

1. By yielding to the Holy Spirit

Yielding to the voice and leading of the Holy Spirit guarantees a leader's development into a wholesome lifestyle that makes him beam with the glow of Christ's countenance under all circumstances. Such a life enjoys the rest of God and operates out of that rest.

To yield is to surrender total control to the Holy Spirit to be guided right. We can be mislead by our inconsistent emotions, confused minds, undisciplined wills, changing circumstances; personalities stronger than ours; mounting pressures and outside influences. Our safety lies in yielding to the Holy Spirit within. Besides that being a safe course to take, there is the full assurance that we shall reach our destination and accomplish our goal on time.

Our only salvation from torturous guessing is to be sensitive to the leading of the Holy Spirit in every minute detail of our lives. It is a great joy to know we can be led by the Holy Spirit, consciously or unconsciously.

Several times I have experienced the unconscious leading of the Holy Spirit when talking to total strangers about something. During or at the end of the conversation I was told this was the answer from God that they were seeking. I am prone to believe that God often works in us and through us, even when we may be unconscious of His workings. We become supernaturally natural in everything we do to the measure that Christ is formed in us, and that is where He finds full expression through us.

Speaker in season brings God's answer

I was visiting a place that was totally strange to me. I was enjoying being in the meetings when suddenly I was asked to speak. This was a surprise to me as I was not scheduled to speak. After speaking, the Spirit of the Lord came upon me mightily. I began to prophecy over individuals, and the anointing lasted from 10:00 p.m. until 1:00 a.m.. The presence of God was mighty. The anointing was rich and evident to all, and flowing with the spirit of prophecy. There were confirmations to many of what God was saying to them, and some of them were of a serious nature.

One such revelation was the revealing of a conversation that took place between two leading brethren of the institution. The words were repeated verbatim. The subject that was discussed by them was revealed. They both were seeking the leading of the Holy Spirit as to whether or not their senior leader should go to a certain country where trouble had been brewing.

They were, however, unable to ascertain the will of God. After the Holy Spirit reiterated their conversation and concerns, He said, "It is not the will of God for you to go, for war will erupt suddenly in that country." The next day war did erupt. When we miss God it creates messes that are very costly.❏

We must learn to wait upon the Lord and to be attentive to His voice and sensitive to His leading.

Principle	*Comment*

146. The role of the Holy Spirit is to conform us into Christ's likeness in behavior and performance so that we obey Him explicitly.

- Loving obedience affects the greatest changes in life. It makes us pliable in His hand and easy to make progressive changes.

2 Corinthians 4:16 (NKJV)   Therefore we do not lose heart. Even though our outward man is perishing, yet the inward man is being renewed day by day.

---

147. As he yields to the Holy Spirit to work in him greater enlargement by God's grace, a sincere leader continues to be more aware of his desperate need, causing him to bend and become the example for others to follow.

- Total awareness of our need brings total yieldedness, resulting in total change. Progress toward a set goal demands constant change. When we welcome constant change we enjoy continual progress.

Psalm 18:19 (NKJV)   He also brought me out into a broad place; He delivered me because He delighted in me.

Principle	*Comment*

148. The leader who realizes that the best way to prove godliness is by Christlikeness, continues to yield to the leadings and dealings of the Holy Spirit to bring forth the full expression of Christ in his life.

- Our safety lies in our total yieldedness to the operations of the Spirit of God. He is the divine agent of transformation that causes us to change from within. Inner transformation brings forth progressive change.

Romans 8:29 (NKJV)   For whom He foreknew, He also predestined to be conformed to the image of His Son, that He might be the firstborn among many brethren.

149. A leader who constantly yields to the Holy Spirit will make tremendous strides from cruelty to kindness, from foolishness to wisdom, and from ugliness of disposition to gentleness.

- Yielding constantly brings forth a transformation for the best. Becoming like Christ is by an inner process not by outward pressure and legislation, and not by the laws and the traditions of men that tend to oppress.

Colossians 1:13 (NKJV)   He has delivered us from the power of darkness and conveyed us into the kingdom of the Son of His love,

Principle	*Comment*
150. When the Spirit of Christ is prevailing in a leader He produces a Christlike character both in him and in those to whom he is ministering; this is the need of the hour in our generation.	• We become like the spirit we imbibe. Christ's Spirit creates in us His pure motives and right attitudes leading us to be a full expression of Himself. This is God's ultimate in redemption that pleases Him most.

2 Corinthians 3:18 (NKJV) But we all, with unveiled face, beholding as in a mirror the glory of the Lord, are being transformed into the same image from glory to glory, just as by the Spirit of the Lord.

2. By continual personal improvement

A leader must apply two principles that make him what he ought to be. First, he must examine himself daily to find out where he's failing or where he is excelling. (1 Corinthians 11:28) Second, he must judge himself and mend any defective areas he discovers. (1 Corinthians 11:31) Sound business principles thrive on periodic stock taking (inventory).

Leader's success based on mentor's wisdom

A leader was asked how he was able to keep his relationship and walk with God intact. They also wanted to know how he ran his operation so smoothly, free from all discrepancies that plague many businesses. This was his reply, "When I was young I attached myself to a mature and wise leader who was rich in experiences, to learn how to be wise. I read in the book of Proverbs, 'He who walks with the wise shall be wise.' I learned to submit to his advice and counsel. I learned to listen to his corrections and warnings. This has saved me many reversals in life and prevented me from having unnecessary headaches."

"He taught me that honesty leads to transparency."

"For transparency to be maintained I had to do two things daily. At the end of each day I must examine myself according to 1 Corinthians 11:28. He taught me to be daring in facing myself so I could be delivered from cowardice. He said, 'Keep your slate clean between you and the Lord, between you and yourself, and between you and others. Examine your spirit, motives, attitudes, thoughts, words, actions, and also your reactions. Then humble yourself before God always and ask Him to forgive you where you have failed. Ask God to teach you how to come up to His high standard by His grace.'"

"The second thing he taught me was to judge myself according to 1 Corinthians 11:31. It is better that we judge ourselves than wait to be judged by others. We make better and faster progress that way. To do this we must always be aware of our accountability to God."

"It only takes a neglected small hole to sink a big ship. The pressure of the water usually enlarges a hole gradually until it is discovered too late. It is the small foxes that spoil the vine. They have a habit of growing fast, and so do small sins. Little weeds, unless plucked, grow fast and choke the entire crop. He taught me never to make excuses for my failures; but, in every failure learn to humble myself before the Lord, seek His help, and mend my ways."❏

Judgment is the secret to progress in life. Let us do it willingly and consistently.

Principle	*Comment*
151. The leader who desires his followers to be like himself, continually improves his character, as well as his administrative ability.	• Building a strong foundation guarantees a sure superstructure. Wholesome character precedes dynamic performance.

Proverbs 19:20 (NKJV) Listen to counsel and receive instruction, that you may be wise in your latter days.

Principle	**_Comment_**
152. Every leader must take time to be with the people God has called him to lead, to become mutually acquainted and to develop more fully the qualities he needs in his leadership.	• There is mutual gain in being sociable with others. It sets the stage for interaction and mutual edification in an atmosphere of friendliness. Loving expressions leave indelible impressions.

Romans 1:11 (NKJV)   For I long to see you, that I may impart to you some spiritual gift, so that you may be established;

---

153. The leader who endeavors to continually modify his behavior will automatically influence the behavior of his followers by his example.	• Leaders who welcome continual discipline in their lives, mature progressively and enjoy having and exhibiting a Christlike disposition.

1 Corinthians 9:27 (NIV)   No, I beat my body and make it my slave so that after I have preached to others, I myself will not be disqualified for the prize.

Principle	*Comment*
154. A leader who always endeavors to be his best and to do his best, will find that his example compels others to follow in his footsteps.	• The greatest compelling force in life is a godly example; it exemplifies divine qualities that draw people to Christ. The process of becoming like Christ is costly but most rewarding.

Philippians 3:14 (NKJV)   I press toward the goal for the prize of the upward call of God in Christ Jesus.

---

155. A leader who incorporates the truth he hears and reads into his practical life daily, makes great progress as an example for others to follow.	• As leaders grow so will their people; they determine the rate of growth in their people at various stages in life. Our growth rate is determined by the measure of our discipline.

1 Timothy 4:15 (NKJV)   Meditate on these things; give yourself entirely to them, that your progress may be evident to all.

Principle	*Comment*

156. When the leader heeds what he learns, he lives to be the best example.

- He who takes the advice he gives others gains great rewards.

Proverbs 15:32 (NKJV)   He who disdains instruction despises his own soul, but he who heeds rebuke gets understanding.

157. It is of great importance that a leader pay proper attention to his own personal appearance. By a marked increase in tidiness, he gains the respect of all.

- He who represents the King must look kingly. Proper attire and well-groomed hair are befitting a leader. Conforming to the world leaves leaders looking shabby and wild.

Genesis 41:14 (NKJV)   Then Pharaoh sent and called Joseph, and they brought him quickly out of the dungeon; and he shaved, changed his clothing, and came to Pharaoh.

Principle	**Comment**
158. Until a leader declares war against an evil habit that enslaves him rendering him ineffective, he cannot be his best for God or be of any use to man.	• The cycle of obsession that forms habits must be broken, lest he be rendered helpless in accomplishing his goal. Habits go from being strings, to ropes, to steel cables.

1 Peter 4:1-2 (NKJV) Therefore, since Christ suffered for us in the flesh, arm yourselves also with the same mind, for he who has suffered in the flesh has ceased from sin, {2} that he no longer should live the rest of his time in the flesh for the lusts of men, but for the will of God.

| 159. The leader who is a slave to destructive habits disqualifies himself for the role of leadership, which demands being an example others can follow. | • Slavery to bad habits has disqualified many leaders from their role. A bad habit is a choice we make that we can break by God's grace and power. |

Romans 6:12-13 (NKJV) Therefore do not let sin reign in your mortal body, that you should obey it in its lusts. {13} And do not present your members as instruments of unrighteousness to sin, but present yourselves to God as being alive from the dead, and your members as instruments of righteousness to God.

---

3. By tests and experiences

Tests of all kinds are necessary for continual progress in character development as well as in performance. Experiences are a conglomeration of happenings we go through in life that teach us the valuable lessons that contribute to our growth. Experience is a unique teacher; it gives the test first, then afterward it teaches the lesson. Experience is compulsory education for everyone alike. We retain those lessons that we learn from the costly experiences in life.

Well-timed charge wins the battle

A kingdom was being invaded by an overpowering neighboring king. The king who was being attacked called upon an old, well-experienced retired general who had been sorely tested in past wars that he had won. The general was to advise him on the spot in battle. When the two armies were lined up against each other ready for the signal to attack, the commander of the invading forces gave orders to the drummer to beat the drums. The drummer did the first beat and waited for a minute. He did the second beat and waited for another minute. Then he did the third beat, but nothing happened.

When the king heard the first beat of the invading drum he attempted to give the same signal to his own drummer. He wanted to give his beat so his forces would charge. However, to his surprise, the general restrained him until the other drummer finished his third beat. He than allowed the king to give his signal for his drummer to beat only once, and give the charge. They won the battle easily.

The king inquired regarding the general's advice, "Why did you restrain me from giving the signal for our drummer to beat?" The general said, "Experience taught us again and again, that at the first beat the soldier's courage is at its peak and so is their morale. This makes it the best time to charge. Hesitancy between one beat and another drains a soldier's courage, brings fear, and causes tension that paralyses a soldier's concentration. Experience has taught us that it is courage at its height that wins wars."❏

Tests and experiences of the past can teach us much through people who have paid the price to go through them in life.

Principle	*Comment*
160. The Lord knows what kind of pressure to bring to bear upon every leader to develop in him divine qualities, which bring forth an expression of Himself.	• Everything in life is tested by pressure, including leaders. God uses inner and outward pressures to the degree needed for our development.

Job 23:10 (NKJV)   But He knows the way that I take; when He has tested me, I shall come forth as gold.

Principle	*Comment*
161. Sensible leaders will not resist going through what God has ordained for them —to make them what they ought to be.	• Knowing the price of becoming such a leader they accumulate experiences, which become a vital part of their lives, and thus they teach by example.

1 Peter 4:19 (NIV)   So then, those who suffer according to God's will should commit themselves to their faithful Creator and continue to do good.

---

162. Every leader has his brightest hour and his darkest hour; how he reacts to them reveals his caliber.	• It is in the darkest hours that we are severely tested. Everyone reacts differently to their midnight experiences.

Acts 16:25 (NKJV)   But at midnight Paul and Silas were praying and singing hymns to God, and the prisoners were listening to them.

Principle	*Comment*
163. Victorious leaders get through even the hardest journey by taking only one step at a time, and asking for God's strength to keep on going.	• Victory is always sure when leaders rely totally on the Lord. Leaders who derive their strength from Him enjoy victorious living.

Philippians 4:12-13 (NKJV)   I know how to be abased, and I know how to abound. Everywhere and in all things I have learned both to be full and to be hungry, both to abound and to suffer need. {13} I can do all things through Christ who strengthens me.

---

164. No adverse circumstance, difficult test, or harsh trial can do any harm to a leader who exemplifies the character of God in his reactions.	• When we are deeply rooted in God nothing affects us but God Himself. What we go through serves His purpose.

1 Peter 1:7 (NKJV)   that the genuineness of your faith, being much more precious than gold that perishes, though it is tested by fire, may be found to praise, honor, and glory at the revelation of Jesus Christ,

---

Principle	*Comment*
165. A leader endowed with divine wisdom, knows how to tactfully surmount difficulties and maneuver his way through obstacles to reach his destination without hurting himself or others.	• Divine wisdom gives us the ways and means to wade through difficulties and overcome obstacles successfully. It is the secret of accomplishing great things in spite of all the contrarinesses along the way.

Proverbs 2:10-11 (NKJV)   When wisdom enters your heart, and knowledge is pleasant to your soul, {11} discretion will preserve you; understanding will keep you,

---

166. Since the test of good behavior is being able to endure bad behavior, a leader must be an example for others to follow in this respect.	• Good behavior is consistent in the face of the worst; it is a life that draws its sap from the eternal resources of God.

Ephesians 4:2 (NKJV)   with all lowliness and gentleness, with longsuffering, bearing with one another in love,

Principle	*Comment*
167. When leaders stop reacting to the actions of others and express Christ in His fullness, regardless of the circumstances in which they find themselves, they will make perpetual progress.	• When Christ controls our lives, we control our circumstances, and affect the necessary changes needed at every interval of life. Leaders who are influenced by Christ will not be influenced by the world.

1 Thessalonians 5:15 (NKJV)   See that no one renders evil for evil to anyone, but always pursue what is good both for yourselves and for all.

168. A variety of experiences in many fields make a leader a shining object to be sought after by colleagues and followers alike as they see in him a resourceful and valuable person from which to draw.	• He who desires to reach the heights must stay up late at night studying ardently—not watching television. Diligence characterizes the life of leaders who aim at excellence through persistency of purpose.

Daniel 12:3 (NKJV)   Those who are wise shall shine like the brightness of the firmament, and those who turn many to righteousness like the stars forever and ever.

4. By taking the lead and setting the pace

A confident leader leads with sure steps and a clear purpose. He charts the course to his destination with cheerfulness and rest in his spirit.

A leader is not qualified to lead unless he is first led by the Lord. Every leader should wait for God's confirmation before he sets the pace for his people to follow. Knowing God intimately sensitizes a leader to His Spirit. It awakens in him every sleeping atom to respond to the Spirit of God.

Business saved as Spirit-led leader takes the helm

A young leader was approached by the president of a large operation to consider taking his position. The young man was shocked and asked, "Why did you choose me when I am younger than you are and less experienced?"

The president answered, "Due to many pressures within my family, in the business, and from my peers, I have lost my sensitivity to the leading of the Holy Spirit. I began to make major decisions that are vital to the operation out of my reasoning, based on my past experiences, only to discover they were all wrong. Now I do not know the answer to the situation. I do not know whether to totally close down an operation that was once very successful under my predecessor, or hand it over to someone else."

"Now to answer your question. I observed the way you operate where you are. Deep in my heart I sense that you are a godly man. You seek the Lord. You take time to wait upon God, and God leads you in every step you take. That is why you are prospering in a way that is outstanding to all concerned." The young man accepted the offer after he prayed and felt a strong witness of the Holy Spirit. This was confirmed several times over.

The operation was in shambles. Everything needed to be over-hauled. As he sought the leading of the Lord in every step to be taken, the Lord instructed him how to proceed. It took time, but the operation recovered, became successful again and excelled.☐

He who is attentive to God will hear His voice without the need of an amplifier. He who moves with God will find His provision sufficient for every step he takes. It behooves us to ascertain the will of God, then move swiftly, wisely, and confidently to implement it for His glory.

Principle	*Comment*
169. A leader can expect his people to do only what he himself has been able to do.	• Seeing propels doing. What inspires the eye motivates the will into action.

Matthew 23:4 (NKJV)   "For they bind heavy burdens, hard to bear, and lay them on men's shoulders; but they themselves will not move them with one of their fingers."

---

170. A successful leader is one who leads the way by first doing the very things he expects his followers to do.	• A leader must pay the highest price in self-denial and self-discipline to affect his followers.

John 13:14-15 (NKJV)   "If I then, your Lord and Teacher, have washed your feet, you also ought to wash one another's feet. {15} For I have given you an example, that you should do as I have done to you."

Principle	*Comment*
171. Leaders must lead the way in everything, to help their people accomplish the will and the plan of God.	• Humility leads to initiative and results in progress. A leader whose steps are precise and clearly defined is a pleasure to follow.

1 Peter 2:21 (NKJV) For to this you were called, because Christ also suffered for us, leaving us an example, that you should follow His steps:

| 172. Skillful people lead the way in their field becoming leaders that others love to follow. | • Total dedication in training produces skillfulness in performance. |

Daniel 1:4 (NKJV) young men in whom there was no blemish, but good-looking, gifted in all wisdom, possessing knowledge and quick to understand, who had ability to serve in the king's palace, and whom they might teach the language and literature of the Chaldeans.

Principle	*Comment*

173. A leader who knows that he must take the initiative when something needs to be done, does not shove off his responsibility on others, but takes the lead in each venture enlisting their cooperation.

- Decisive leaders take the initiative in the right direction and move directly into action. Such leaders enjoy ardent followers who behold their sure steps leading to their set goal.

Judges 18:9 (NKJV)   So they said, "Arise, let us go up against them. For we have seen the land, and indeed it is very good. Would you do nothing? Do not hesitate to go, and enter to possess the land."

174. The leader who is a pace-setter will be followed more easily than an undecided one.

- Making decisions and implementing them is one of the greatest challenges to leaders.

Acts 16:10 (NKJV)   Now after he had seen the vision, immediately we sought to go to Macedonia, concluding that the Lord had called us to preach the gospel to them.

Principle	**Comment**
175. An encouraged leader sets the pace for his followers by carefully guarding them against discouragement.	• There is no room for discouragement in God. It is Satan's "stop sign" against progress. It is a wrong response to a lying spirit.

1 Thessalonians 2:11-12 (NKJV)   as you know how we exhorted, and comforted, and charged every one of you, as a father does his own children, {12} that you would walk worthy of God who calls you into His own kingdom and glory.

5. By helping others to do their best

A helpful leader imparts his expertise to his people with calmness and ease and challenges them to yield their maximum effort to accomplish their set goal.

It is much easier to offer advice than help. Some people feel sorry for others in need. Instead they need to help them meet their need. He who helps others out of trouble stays out of trouble himself.

Leader stays small to help others succeed

A knowledgeable, richly experienced leader had a small operation going on that never grew big. He was asked the reason for that. He said, "I have a settled conviction that it is far better for me to grow the best in others, to produce my best in others, and to help them to succeed, than for only me to succeed by myself and becoming big."❑

He who does not give his best in life lives to feel the worst. He who aims at excellence will produce excellence in others and reap better dividends in the long run.

Inspiring people to reach the height of their potential, to motivate them to take the initiative to move daringly, and to challenge them to persist until they reach their set goal, is a great and rewarding experience for the wise.

Sacrificing on behalf of others is the proof of true love that lives on without quitting or any thought of recompense. Selfishness short-circuits life and tarnishes everything it touches.

Principle	*Comment*
176. There is a great difference between a boss and a leader. While a boss may command his people to perform, a leader works with them, helping them to do their best by doing his best. He is a continual inspiration to all.	• When people are inspired, they don't have to be commanded. It is easy for them to be motivated to action and move with their leader. They give their full cooperation willingly, which yields great results.

2 Corinthians 1:24 (NIV) Not that we lord it over your faith, but we work with you for your joy, because it is by faith you stand firm.

---

177. A loving leader relaxes his people by his example, dissipating their fears. They don't even fear making mistakes, knowing that he will help them, rather than scold them.	• Restoration, rather than condemnation, should be the aim of leaders. Training people to fulfill their calling includes bearing with their failures. Failure is a revelation of an unmet need.

Galatians 6:1 (NKJV) Brethren, if a man is overtaken in any trespass, you who are spiritual restore such a one in a spirit of gentleness, considering yourself lest you also be tempted.

Principle	*Comment*

178. When a leader adopts the theme of "Be encouraged, I am here and will back you up even when you fail," he becomes the leading example in lifting up the spirits of the failing ones onto a higher plateau for a fresh start, undaunted.

- An example is a load-lifter with the ministry of assurance of total support. He is always ready to lend his shoulder, his talents, his giftings, his experiences, and even his purse when needed. With a leader of such caliber people will lay down their life for him.

Luke 22:32 (NKJV)   "But I have prayed for you, that your faith should not fail; and when you have returned to Me, strengthen your brethren."

179. An exemplary leader is willing to take the blame for the failures of his followers, regardless of the cost, and help mend the situation in the best way possible.

- Some leaders are willing to take only the praise and so fall short of being an example. When heavy loads are shared they become light. Blame is always laid on leaders, regardless of who failed in their operation.

1 Peter 4:8 (NKJV)   And above all things have fervent love for one another, for "love will cover a multitude of sins."

Principle	***Comment***
180. A leader must learn to walk with the afflicted through the valley of sorrow, pain, and hardship, with gentleness of spirit like his Master, to win their affection and help bring healing to them.	• Gentleness is stronger than force; it motivates the will to move and releases all inner forces. It is a necessary attribute that enlivens a leader's life. The quality of a strong character is fortified by the unmatched force of its gentleness.

Isaiah 53:3 (NKJV)   He is despised and rejected by men, a Man of sorrows and acquainted with grief. And we hid, as it were, our faces from Him; He was despised, and we did not esteem Him.

---

181. The leader who walks where his people walk will be able to gain their confidence and will find it easier to relate to them.	• Humility always wins the heart of God and man. Those who travel on the pathway of Christ won't find the traffic congested.

Philippians 2:1-3 (NKJV)   Therefore if there is any consolation in Christ, if any comfort of love, if any fellowship of the Spirit, if any affection and mercy, {2} fulfill my joy by being like-minded, having the same love, being of one accord, of one mind. {3} Let nothing be done through selfish ambition or conceit, but in lowliness of mind let each esteem others better than himself.

B. HINDRANCES to Development

Selfishness, self-sparing, fears, compromise, and lack of total dedication stymie a leader's development to the fullest extent and abort the process. A life yielded to the Spirit of God develops God's attributes by applying divine principles to come up to God's standard.

Selfishness is indicative of self-love. Self-sparing indicates a lack of commitment. Fear is indicative of a lack of simplicity of faith in God's ability and dependability. And compromise shows him to be a man-pleaser rather than a God-pleaser.

Gifted evangelist takes over church, kicks pastor out

An evangelist who was gifted with signs, wonders, and miracles, came to the largest church in the largest city in a state. God blessed his ministry greatly, and instead of giving God all the glory and praise, it went to his head and he thought to himself, "How great am I," rather than, "Lord, How great Thou art!" All of God's gifts are entrusted to us to fulfill His will and purpose, and give Him all the glory.

Developing our God-given gifts but neglecting to build an exemplary character is dangerous to the gifted and to his followers. When a head swells beyond its fullest capacity, it explodes. This gifted brother became obsessed with the selfish thought of taking over the church and kicking out the pastor, which he did to the shock of everyone. God withdrew His presence and the successful work came to a halt.❏

Selfishness lays the groundwork for deception to set in and gives a place to the Devil to work. Walking with God supersedes serving Him. Foundation precedes building the superstructure. It is costly to embrace the cross with all its transforming operations to develop an exemplary character. Gifts are bestowed upon us to equip us to operate according to the dictates of the Holy Spirit.

When we use God's gifts for selfish gain we quench and grieve the Holy Spirit, the gifts lie dormant, and we lose out with God. We create a confidence crisis that disillusions the once enamored followers, and we wake up to find ourselves alone and lonely. Unless we take our walk with God seriously, we don't consider our accountability to Him as a fearful thing.

1. Not allowing God to be total master of our life

An arrogant leader takes the lead independent of God due to the pride of his heart. Missing His way results in creating messes and hurting the people involved. No leader can be the master of his fate and hope to succeed in his mission. A leader's success depends on doing things in God's will and in His way, time, and place.

Pride violates divine principles and blocks the avenue of revelation. Lack of acknowledging the supremacy of God over our lives and refusal to submit to His leading, end up in independent acts that violate divine principles. This will culminate in judgment.

Rebel son usurps the throne but loses his life

A king had ruled his kingdom for many years, peacefully and prosperously. He groomed his eldest son who was heir to the throne. The eldest son proved himself to be trustworthy and all was going well. His younger brother, however, was rebellious, living away from home, full of pride and arrogance. He came home motivated to take over the reins of the kingdom. He attacked his brother, shot him in the head, and took over the kingdom. This was done to the dismay of all the citizens and the grief of his old father.

One of the generals was loyal to the father and to the eldest son. He came to the elderly king and sat beside his bed to consult with him regarding their loyalty to the new self-appointed king who usurped the throne. The old king's words were spoken slowly, carefully, but forcefully. "As much as I love my son, I will not allow personal consideration to prevail over justice and righteousness. Pride must be dealt with by death and there is no other way." His orders were carried out immediately.❏

When God leads the way, it is with love, peace, wisdom, and safety. All independent acts stem out of selfish gain, and many are hurt in the process. God deliver us from such.

Principle	*Comment*
182. Leaders who compromise their conviction, their strong stand, and their identification with Christ and God's standard, because of fear of criticism, fail to become the example others follow. They also lose the confidence of those who once admired them in their leadership role.	• Compromisers are the greatest losers. There are several reasons for compromise, the worst of which is an imbedded insecurity due to a defective relationship with God. Where there is a strong relationship with God established through total submission to His revealed will it fortifies a leader's character.

1 Samuel 15:24 (NKJV)   Then Saul said to Samuel, "I have sinned, for I have transgressed the commandment of the LORD and your words, because I feared the people and obeyed their voice."

Principle	*Comment*
183. It is unfair for a leader who cannot conquer his own body—with all its cravings and appetites—to lead others for two reasons: first, he follows his uncrucified desires rather than masters them; second, he is not being a good example.	• Embracing the cross and all its operations is the only means by which to conquer. The cross is the greatest saving factor from the enslavement of lustful desires. Leaders who welcome the death side of the cross enjoy the resurrection side greatly.

Galatians 5:16 (NKJV)   I say then: Walk in the Spirit, and you shall not fulfill the lust of the flesh.

---

184. It is a grave mistake for any leader to live by God's alternatives, which were given to man because of the hardness of his heart. To live by alternatives reveals hidden rebellion.	• Only escapists live by alternatives. Those who are sincere, love God's principles and always apply them, even under severe circumstances. They don't settle for less than God's perfect will, regardless of the price.

Matthew 19:8 (NKJV)   He said to them, "Moses, because of the hardness of your hearts, permitted you to divorce your wives, but from the beginning it was not so."

Principle	*Comment*

185. The leader who does not express Christ's life in his daily walk does not have much to offer, even though he may be most eloquent.

- Christ came to impart the very life of the Father and expects its manifestation through our yieldedness. He meant for us to be the full expression of the Father as He was.

Galatians 2:20 (NIV) I have been crucified with Christ and I no longer live, but Christ lives in me. The life I live in the body, I live by faith in the Son of God, who loved me and gave himself for me.

186. The leader who does not meet God early, following the example of his Lord, has a serious problem with mixed priorities.

- Unless Christ has the pre-eminence in a leader's life, he is in continual trouble. When Jesus is Lord, He becomes the determining factor.

Psalm 5:3 (NKJV) My voice You shall hear in the morning, O LORD; in the morning I will direct it to You, and I will look up.

2. Harboring carnality

Carnality degrades a leader's life, jeopardizes his position, deforms his character, and creates a confidence crisis. No leader can lead effectively without having the confidence of his people. It is the unguarded moment that reveals our hidden carnality. The crises of life exhibit the qualities of our character.

Life is built on laws that govern all of its movements with precision. One of those outstanding laws is the law of sowing and reaping, namely reciprocity. There is no fleeing from consequences in life. The illegal pleasure of the moment that deceives us has its eternal consequences that confront us. He who is wise thinks the farthest in life; but, he who is wisest thinks beyond this life to eternity.

Indulging in carnality to gratify fleshly desires reaps its "sour grapes," which embitters life and drives it to utter despair. The more a person sins the more sin puts its forceful demands toward accelerating the sinning. Sin drives people out of their minds through deception to cause them to do things that cater to their whims. This will eventually destroy them. Yielding is a choice, whether to good or to evil. We make our own choices. Then our choices make us as we live by them.

Leader overcomes sexual assault with God's help

I was visiting a leader in a nearby country, who is responsible for a huge successful operation. He was enjoying wide acceptance and the cooperation of many people from various levels in the community. He related to me this story.

Two women who belonged to his operation had agreed together to give themselves to him in an illicit manner. This was shocking to him. They arrived at his office when he was alone doing his preparation. He asked them why they had come. They bluntly said that they were "after" him. They attacked him and began to strip him forcefully. He said to me, "I am strong physically and I would never think anyone could overpower me, but I was almost to that point. I had to call aloud on the name of the Lord to help me. Suddenly the Spirit of God came upon me mightily and I was able to throw them out of the scene completely." Thank God for His deliverance.❑

Holy determination to make the right choices enables a leader to conquer in every battle of life.

Principle	*Comment*
187. The leader afflicted with a violent and rebellious streak that always defies authority, should not be surprised when others follow his pattern—manifesting the same attitudes, backfiring on him.	• The law of reciprocity operates day and night without fail. It is a most powerful law, that operates without respect to position or status. Like begets like. Every one produces after his own kind.

Psalm 68:6 (NKJV)   God sets the solitary in families; He brings out those who are bound into prosperity; but the rebellious dwell in a dry land.

Principle	**Comment**
188. The leader who thinks he can hide his ugly disposition with smart eloquence and fluent words, is sinking deeper into deception, for his life speaks louder than his words.	• No one can fool all the people all of the time; he's bound to get caught. Mistreating others and degrading their dignity is easily discerned and terribly detested. Refined leaders treat people with excellence.

2 Timothy 2:16 (NKJV)   But shun profane and idle babblings, for they will increase to more ungodliness.

---

189. No leader is safe for long when pride fills his heart and rules his life; woe to those who follow after him, for he shall lead them to the path of death.	• The proud person is detestable to God, to himself, and to others. Pride is self in its worst disposition. He who is full of himself has no room for God.

Proverbs 16:18 (NKJV)   Pride goes before destruction, and a haughty spirit before a fall.

Principle	*Comment*
190. Retaliation hurts leaders more than insults, accusations, and the criticism they receive; it never works, even with the smartest leader, because it violates divine principles and deprives them from being good examples to follow.	• Vengeance belongs to God; forgiveness is our only recourse. There are three distinct marks of the Christian life: loving, giving, and forgiving. Loving regardless of their status, giving regardless of their need, and forgiving regardless of their failure.

Romans 12:19 (NIV)   Do not take revenge, my friends, but leave room for God's wrath, for it is written: "It is mine to avenge; I will repay," says the Lord.

—————————————

| 191. The leadership role has suffered greatly from its "Judahs", who are starters, but are victimized by selfishness along the way, and never finish. | • Finishers are credited highly for their outstanding accomplishments. They pay the highest price, but also reap the greatest dividends. |

Luke 14:28-29 (NKJV)   "For which of you, intending to build a tower, does not sit down first and count the cost, whether he has enough to finish it; {29} lest, after he has laid the foundation, and is not able to finish, all who see it begin to mock him,"

—————————————

Principle	*Comment*

192. Some leaders are rich in revelation of truth, but fail to convey their hearts to the people due to their insensitivity.

- The more we value people as God does, the more we become sensitive to their feelings and thoughtful to their needs.

Ephesians 4:17-19 (NIV)   So I tell you this, and insist on it in the Lord, that you must no longer live as the Gentiles do, in the futility of their thinking. {18} They are darkened in their understanding and separated from the life of God because of the ignorance that is in them due to the hardening of their hearts. {19} Having lost all sensitivity, they have given themselves over to sensuality so as to indulge in every kind of impurity, with a continual lust for more.

---

193. To walk in forbidden paths is strictly prohibited for leaders who desire to be an example in their walk before God and man.

- The forbidden hurts us most and is a warning from God, who wants the best for us and from us. God only forbids what hurts us.

Hebrews 12:13 (NKJV)   and make straight paths for your feet, so that what is lame may not be dislocated, but rather be healed.

Principle	*Comment*
194. A stained leader will find it hard to leave an indelible mark for good on his people.	• Broken character is hard to mend—it is like the glass that shows the cracks.

2 Peter 2:18 (NKJV)   For when they speak great swelling words of emptiness, they allure through the lusts of the flesh, through lewdness, the ones who have actually escaped from those who live in error.

3. Instructing without leading

An instructor verbalizes his instructions while a leader leads the way and makes it easy for his people to follow his example with ease and confidence. People will go as far as they can see their leader go. Neither instructions nor authoritative commands can take the place of mature leadership.

Winning general sends instructions to battle and loses

A tired and exhausted general exempted himself from leading his troops in the final battle. He thought that since they had won every preceding battle he could give the necessary instructions on how to proceed and win the final one. He had forgotten that people follow a leader whom they see much better than instructions that they hear.

Suffice it to say that they lost the war by losing the last battle. He who wins the final battle usually wins the war.❏

Leadership is an integral part of life in all of its aspects. It is as necessary as breathing air. The dearth of leaders ends up in chaos, utter confusion, and defeat. Leadership unifies, strategies, edifies, and amplifies. Instruction can be forgotten. Even if not fully forgotten it will be partially neglected. The understanding of instructions varies. Instructions at their best are no substitute for leadership at its best.

Negligence leads to defeat in life and in performance. Victory belongs to the alert and diligent who pursue their goal with persistency. Victory neither comes automatically nor is it permanent. It must be won, maintained, and well-guarded.

Principle	*Comment*

195. Most men who occupy the role of leadership are instructors rather than leaders, causing many operations to suffer.

- To lead is to go before; to instruct is to impart knowledge. Before we lead we must first be an example.

Romans 2:21-22 (NKJV)   You, therefore, who teach another, do you not teach yourself? You who preach that a man should not steal, do you steal? {22} You who say, "Do not commit adultery," do you commit adultery? You who abhor idols, do you rob temples?

———————

196. The leader who expects his followers to do what he will not do himself puts his name in the archives of the unreasonable. He will finally declare his bankruptcy because of his inability to lead others. The nature of leadership is first to do, then to teach.

- He who lives the truth seeks no exceptions to the rule and thus reveals his uprightness before God and man. Talking is cheap, while doing is expensive; accepting the cross makes all the difference. The cross is the only means for practical progress.

Acts 1:1 (NKJV)   The former account I made, O Theophilus, of all that Jesus began both to do and teach,

———————

4. Lacking positive influence

A negative leader can never have a positive influence on his people. He is bound by his legalistic ways and close-mindedness, which make it hard for him to receive input. His clouded vision restricts him from seeing and enjoying the sun. He is like a night owl that sees everything dark. Positive influence can turn stagnant people into active people who will excel in their pursuit of excellence.

Rude top administrator transmits negative influence

There once was a man who was a skilled administrator over a large and significant Institution where students attended from all over the world. The staff and instructors were among the best. Students came from various places to study God's Word and to prepare for ministry. On one hand, this skilled administrator was highly degreed. On the other hand, he lacked positive influence because he was often insensitive, rude, and even harsh in the way he treated his subordinates.

His problem was evident to all. He failed to establish and operate out of relationship. He operated out of position with a domineering spirit, which caused the institute's spiritual morale to sink to a low ebb—forcing him to resign. Unless respect, kindness, and integrity characterize a leader's disposition, he fails to relate to his people in a healthy and inspiring manner.❏

Principle	*Comment*
197. As a leader's shadow is closest to him, so is his influence for better or for worse.	• Our rise and fall is dependent on how close or how far we are from God.

Exodus 17:9 (NKJV)   And Moses said to Joshua, "Choose us some men and go out, fight with Amalek. Tomorrow I will stand on the top of the hill with the rod of God in my hand."

| 198. The leader whose influence does not carry far, especially among his own people, is unfit to continue in his post. | • Mixture in life dissipates one's influence. Influence is a stamp that is birthed in the womb of an exemplary life. |

1 Kings 15:1-3 (NKJV)   In the eighteenth year of King Jeroboam the son of Nebat, Abijam became king over Judah. {2} He reigned three years in Jerusalem. His mother's name was Maachah the granddaughter of Abishalom. {3} And he walked in all the sins of his father, which he had done before him; his heart was not loyal to the LORD his God, as was the heart of his father David.

Principle	*Comment*
199. Long-term stagnation in any operation is due to long-term leadership with a limited vision.	• Progressive vision demands revolutionary changes in the leaders first.

Proverbs 29:18 (NKJV)   Where there is no revelation, the people cast off restraint; but happy is he who keeps the law.

IV. The PRICE

A. The Price of being an Exemplary Leader

Transparency before God, man, angels, and demons is most essential to becoming an exemplary leader ("...no part dark..." Luke 11:36, nkjv). Walking before God and man requires going through the crucible daily. The highest cost of becoming an example is an absolute must on a "cash and carry basis." Every step is scrutinized by God and man. The thorny road to divine fulfillment and greatness in God necessitates our welcoming His price tag with no bargains, sales, or discounts. No wonder Jesus said, "If anyone desires to come after Me, let him deny himself, and take up his cross daily, and follow Me." (Luke 9:23, nkjv) Paul was paying that price daily when he said, "I die daily." (1 Corinthians 15:31, nkjv)

Missionary labors diligently though wife forsakes him

A missionary couple who was dedicated to God and His service arrived at the place of their calling and began to see God in action. His multiplied blessings were overwhelmingly fulfilling the biblical injunction in Deuteronomy 11:26-28 (niv), which is a "blessing if you obey." One day his wife succumbed to temptation and became entangled with a native, and she would not be persuaded otherwise. She divorced her husband, took the children, and went on her wayward way leaving him devastated, to say the least.

He entrusted the matter to the hand of God and pursued his ultimate goal of continual service to Him. His example of keeping a right attitude, being consistent in his relationship with God, and being persistent in laboring diligently for the Lord inspired many of those who beheld his steadfast walk with God to follow in his footsteps. He refused to leave the field, refused to close the door for his wife to return, and rejected the voice of the Devil telling him to become discouraged and end it all by committing suicide.❏

Persistent missionary viciously attacked, wins attacker

Another missionary who was laboring in a country extremely hostile to Christianity used to stand at the gate of the religious training premises, and hand out Gospels to the theological students. One student was greatly incensed by him and warned him not to come back again or he would break his arm that carried the Gospels. He cursed and abused him greatly before everybody. But the missionary persisted in his mission to distribute the Gospel of love, light, and life.

One day the vicious student plotted against him, attacked him, broke his arm and fled. After he was taken to the hospital, he prayed earnestly that the Lord would give him another opportunity to give the Gospel to this student. His persistent and compassionate intercession before God was heard. When we intercede God always intervenes.

The next day he was standing at the gate handing out Gospels with his broken arm in a cast. To his surprise this student came to him and attacked him again, but the missionary lovingly pleaded with him to read a Gospel and judge for himself. It happened to be the Gospel of Mark.

The student consented to the idea and, instead of going to class, he went far away into the desert and read the whole Gospel without stopping, and he was suddenly arrested by the Holy Spirit. He was marvelously saved and came back to tell of his dynamic experience to the missionary. Both embraced each other and worshipped and praised the Lord. Hallelujah.

When the student went home and told the news to his parents, his father was incensed and attempted to kill him until his mother intervened and persuaded the father to put him to death by poisoning him, which he consented to do three times a day for three days. At the end of the third day, the father came to his room and inquired about his son's health. The son replied I feel healthier than ever. Then the father told him about his attempt to kill him silently. At that time the son opened the last chapter of the Gospel of Mark (16:18, kjv) and read, "If they drink any deadly thing, it shall not hurt them." The father broke down and exclaimed, "Your God is the real God. I want Him." Praise the Lord.

The student changed his name to Mark (worshipper of Christ) and changed his studies and became a dynamic servant of God and affected the lives of many through his preaching and writing. All this happened because a dedicated missionary was willing to pay the price of becoming an exemplary leader.❏

1. Willingness to personally bear high cost

Leaders who pay the price get the prize. Total commitment yields the best dividends in the long run. Leadership and sacrifice go together. Leaders who desire to climb the highest must pay the highest price willingly, readily, and delightfully.

Only honest people pay the price. Honesty leads to truthfulness, which results in success.

Nothing in life is free, not even laziness. The lethargic discover too late that the price of lethargy costs more than the price of honesty with diligence.

Man dishonors his family with empty promises

A man got married to a fine lady from a noble family. This marriage gave him status and a place of respectability. It was not long until he revealed his true colors. He was arrogant in spirit, vulgar in his language, terrible in his attitude, and selfish in his mannerisms.

Whenever he picked up his paycheck, he would go to the market and indulge in eating in restaurants until he was full. He would then go home late and miserable, to find his family starving. He would charge his groceries at a nearby shop and promise to pay his bill on payday, but he did not keep his promises.

When pressures to pay mounted high, he moved to a different part of the city, then to a different city, and finally to a different country. He definitely believed in forgiveness. However, it is other people's forgiveness to him. He was a detriment to his family.❑

He who pays the price in embracing the cross gains a place in the heart of people because of his honor in keeping his promises. It pays more than it costs to be honest, truthful, and upright.

Principle	*Comment*
200. If Jesus bypassed the cross, he could not have said, "It is finished." Neither would there be redemption for humanity. All leaders should follow the example of their Grand Master leader.	• Embracing the cross guarantees consistency of purpose and leads to fulfillment. He who has a revelation of the cross glories in it and accepts its transforming operations.

Mark 14:36 (NKJV) And He said, "Abba, Father, all things are possible for You. Take this cup away from Me; nevertheless, not what I will, but what You will."

201. Godly leaders who are committed to Biblical principles often suffer the marks of the cross of Christ, but not in vain, because they will leave a mark on their generation.	• Only committed leaders have hope of becoming examples worthy to be followed. Such leaders spread the aroma of Christ everywhere they go and release His sweet presence.

2 Timothy 3:12 (NKJV) Yes, and all who desire to live godly in Christ Jesus will suffer persecution.

Principle	*Comment*
202. When God calls a leader to be an example, He requires him to pay the highest price and to suffer the most from without and within.	• The price is great, but the dividends are greater. He who welcomes the cross in his life welcomes its promotion—conformity to Christlikeness.

Hebrews 5:8 (NKJV)   though He was a Son, yet He learned obedience by the things which He suffered.

---

203. The leader who is inspired to live by the same ideals as Christ's, which enhance every aspect of his role in leadership, must pay the highest price.	• The enormous price fades away in the light of His likeness. No price that brings us to our ultimate goal is too great when we compare it to the supreme sacrifice.

1 John 2:6 (NKJV)   He who says he abides in Him ought himself also to walk just as He walked.

Principle	*Comment*

204. The leader who realizes "no investment, no gain," invests everything he has to gain something vital.

- We get what we pay for. There are no bargains in the spiritual realm; it operates on a "cash and carry" plan.

Proverbs 13:4 (NKJV) The soul of a lazy man desires, and has nothing; but the soul of the diligent shall be made rich.

---

205. A wise leader knows the fallacy of succeeding in theory but not in practice, and endeavors to close the gap between the two, regardless of the cost.

- Only self-discipline will close the gap. Practicality is the most convincing evidence of a disciplined life—it translates revelation into demonstration.

2 Timothy 2:10 (NKJV) Therefore I endure all things for the sake of the elect, that they also may obtain the salvation which is in Christ Jesus with eternal glory.

2. Scrutiny of followers and others

Exemplary leaders are able to stand the tests from without. They are also ready to stand the sincere scrutiny of their people from within; due to living transparent lives before all.

He that is transparent in his walk with God, fears no man on earth and welcomes the scrutiny of both God and man.

Top leader's high standard revealed amid major scandal

A major scandal was discovered in a large operation that triggered the discovery of minor ones in the lower echelon. The top leader called for the most efficient investigators in his field to do all they could to deal with this problem. Drastic measures had to be taken to rectify the situation, or it would mean the end of the operation.

When the well-experienced investigators arrived they were endowed with sharp discernment. They observed people, their movements, and their insinuations. They knew how to interpret what was being said and could read between the lines. The first thing they asked for was his full cooperation with everyone. He consented and guaranteed them that he would fully cooperate with them in every aspect.

They scrutinized him in a manner that would aggravate anyone in his position. But he remained calm, serene, confident, and transparent, which greatly surprised them.

At the final stage, when they discovered his innocence, they asked him this question, "How do you manage to stay clean and upright when you are handling a billion dollar business with all its loopholes?"

"I always live in the presence of God. Everything I think, say, and do passes His scrutiny first, and upon His approval, I move to act. Transparency before God and man is my motto."

They were stunned to meet someone living in this world who had attained such a high standard. This is what is desperately needed in every strata of life.

They discovered the discrepancies in the company were due to lack of honesty of some of his subordinates. He was able to deal with every one of them in a manner that was terrifying, yet edifying. He did not attack their character. He concentrated on the loopholes and uncovered the weaknesses and defects. He offered them the best godly advice that would edify them. This helped them to learn the lessons out of their failures and to become noble in the quality of their character.❏

God give us more leaders with such refined character.

Principle	*Comment*
206. Leaders are under the scrutiny of their followers, who observe every move they make.	• Whether a leader realizes it or not, he is being watched by God, man, angels, and Satan.

Luke 11:53-54 (NKJV)   And as He said these things to them, the scribes and the Pharisees began to assail Him vehemently, and to cross-examine Him about many things, {54} lying in wait for Him, and seeking to catch Him in something He might say, that they might accuse Him.

Principle	**Comment**
207. The leader who fails to live up to God's standard in his conduct will not pass the test of public scrutiny. It is required of him to have a clean testimony from those who are without and from those who are within.	• Obeying God's principles consistently brings him up to God's standard and satisfies His heart and ours. Wholesome character exhibits divine characteristics that help a leader to flow with love and glow with joy.

1 Timothy 3:2-7 (NKJV)   A bishop then must be blameless, the husband of one wife, temperate, sober-minded, of good behavior, hospitable, able to teach; {3} not given to wine, not violent, not greedy for money, but gentle, not quarrelsome, not covetous; {4} one who rules his own house well, having his children in submission with all reverence {5} (for if a man does not know how to rule his own house, how will he take care of the church of God?); {6} not a novice, lest being puffed up with pride he fall into the same condemnation as the devil. {7} Moreover he must have a good testimony among those who are outside, lest he fall into reproach and the snare of the devil.

Principle	*Comment*
208. Just as a tree is judged by its fruit, so a leader is judged by his behavior, not by his frantic and futile activities.	• Godly relationship is nourished by God and will lack no seasonable fruit; the deeper the roots the more abundant the fruit.

Matthew 7:16 (NKJV) "You will know them by their fruits. Do men gather grapes from thornbushes or figs from thistles?"

209. A leader's decisions determine the course his followers take. If they are born of the Spirit of God, they will lead in the right direction; otherwise, they may be detrimental to the whole operation.	• Leaders who lead in an upright way will have followers who do likewise. God influences people most powerfully through the lives of godly leaders whose rich anointing generates remarkable transforming power.

John 12:50 (NKJV) "And I know that His command is everlasting life. Therefore, whatever I speak, just as the Father has told Me, so I speak."

3. Much is expected of them

The higher the position of leaders, the greater the expectation of their people for them to perform satisfactorily. People look up to their leaders with confidence and revel in their expertise.

Followers always have high expectations of their leaders, and leaders have high expectations of their followers. Life is full of expectations from the time we open our eyes for the day until we close them at night. We live by the expectations we form.

Leaders bring forth the best in their followers when their expectations are high. It releases their loyalty and gives them the impetus to fully cooperate to fulfill their common goal.

Successful, popular leader found bankrupt in character

A leader of a well-recognized operation became very successful and popular due to his being efficient and diligent in his field. Everything, seemingly, was going well when it was discovered that he divorced his wife in a fit of anger. Such a hasty decision shocked everyone.

To their dismay, investigations revealed that he was embezzling an enormous wealth and channeling it outside the country to his account. It was a horrible shock that reverberated far and near.

Honesty, truthfulness, and forthrightness are necessary ingredients in the making of a wholesome leader. He was efficient in his performance but bankrupt in the qualities of his character. In a word, he was a disappointment to all. If he was as upright as he was efficient, his followers' high expectations could have been fulfilled.❏

God give us balanced leaders who know the value of building a strong foundation that will guarantee the building of a strong superstructure.

| *Principle* | *Comment* |

210. Only the best is expected of an exemplary leader who has received and enjoyed God's best.

• A leader who has been exercised in self-discipline has qualified himself to be followed.

Luke 12:48 (NKJV) *"But he who did not know, yet committed things deserving of stripes, shall be beaten with few. For everyone to whom much is given, from him much will be required; and to whom much has been committed, of him they will ask the more."*

211. It pays for a leader to be assertive in confronting important issues that hurt others. Followers usually observe the actions and reactions of their leaders and follow in their footsteps.

• Confrontation is like major surgery, difficult but necessary. To confront is to face a serious issue or a formidable foe with courage. Drastic changes demand outright confrontation.

Galatians 2:11 (NKJV) *Now when Peter had come to Antioch, I withstood him to his face, because he was to be blamed;*

Principle	*Comment*
212. The most demanding position is to be an exemplary leader.	• A leader must always be available to God and man.

James 3:1 (NKJV)   My brethren, let not many of you become teachers, knowing that we shall receive a stricter judgment.

B. The Price of *not being* an Exemplary Leader

Knowledge is costly, but ignorance is more costly. A leader who does not pay the price to gain knowledge, understanding, wisdom, experience, and discipline fails to quality as an exemplary leader. When a leader dodges his responsibility he gives way to early bankruptcy in character, performance, and substance.

No one was born to fail; we fail because of not planning to succeed. Failure is a choice we make. The price of continual failure is self-degradation leading to self-defeat. Leaders who refuse to face up to their obligations will suffer loss of face and place, and will be thrown out of the race.

Worldwide evangelist chooses defeat

A popular leader whose gift of evangelism endeared him worldwide, gained him a big name and a large following, disgraced himself through a hidden weakness that exposed his failure in the public eye twice. He refused to face up to his failure and was forced out of the arena in utter defeat.❏

When we humble ourselves before God in brokenness and wholehearted repentance, we experience God's restoration because of His mercy and abounding grace. A worm is the only thing that cannot stumble. Those who would build high must remain low and go down before God daily to be safe from pride, which causes horrible and embarrassing falls. Self-expression is good; self-control is better; but self-mastery is best.

When we are selfish we become overdosed with pride, which drives us on to the path of fools. Selfishness short-circuits a leader's life and career. Living for self is living in vain, but living for God is the greatest gain.

1. Failure in leadership

We prepare to fail when we fail to prepare to succeed. We succeed only to the degree of our preparation. No one was born a failure. We are what we choose to be at any given time. He who assumes a responsible position without being qualified to perform guarantees his failure. Failures and successes are self-made.

Faked medical diploma leads to many patient deaths

A medical student failed his final exam for graduation. He was known to be lazy, one who wasted time in trivial things, and pleasure-mad. When the final test came he failed miserably because he was not adequately prepared.

Before we can be trusted we must be tested and pass the test.

He could not go back to his country empty-handed. So, he schemed an idea of borrowing his friend's diploma and having a professional printer reproduce a diploma for him with his name on it.

Upon returning home, he enlisted in the army as a medical officer. He was given a high position with a big salary. As time passed it was noticed that most of the patients he treated died. Upon investigation, it was discovered he was a fake, and he paid a high price for it. "Be sure your sin will find you out." (Numbers 32:23, nkjv)❏

Our success in every field of endeavor depends on the measure of our preparation. It was said, "You can fool some of the people some of the time, but you cannot fool all the people all the time." The price of adequate preparation pays enormous dividends. There is no substitute for preparation.

Deception is a temporary success until it is discovered.

Principle	*Comment*
213. The greatest failure among leaders is the one failing to inspire others by his example.	• If a leader's example is a replica of Christ, he inspires, motivates, and challenges others for progress.

1 Thessalonians 2:10-12 (NIV) You are witnesses, and so is God, of how holy, righteous and blameless we were among you who believed. {11} For you know that we dealt with each of you as a father deals with his own children, {12} encouraging, comforting and urging you to live lives worthy of God, who calls you into his kingdom and glory.

---

214. Failing to be a proper example disqualifies a person from being a leader.	• He who pays the highest price to be an example qualifies to be a leader.

1 Samuel 15:26,28 (NKJV) But Samuel said to Saul, "I will not return with you, for you have rejected the word of the LORD, and the LORD has rejected you from being king over Israel." {28} So Samuel said to him, "The LORD has torn the kingdom of Israel from you today, and has given it to a neighbor of yours, who is better than you."

Principle	**Comment**
215. When a leader ceases to be a wholesome example, he becomes a stumbling block affecting both them and himself, resulting in a disastrous end to the whole operation.	• Walking with God is a moment-by-moment yielding that requires consistent discipline in hearing Him attentively, obeying Him promptly, and honoring Him persistently.

Jeremiah 18:15 (NKJV)   "Because My people have forgotten Me, they have burned incense to worthless idols. And they have caused themselves to stumble in their ways, from the ancient paths, to walk in pathways and not on a highway,"

| 216. A mediocre leader does not rank high among his followers. | • A mediocre leader has no respect for himself nor does he have the respect of others. |

Revelation 3:16 (NKJV)   "So then, because you are lukewarm, and neither cold nor hot, I will vomit you out of My mouth."

Principle	*Comment*
217. The leader who does not influence his people spiritually is a failure, regardless of his other qualifications.	• People need the Lord first before all their other many needs. His Lordship over their lives makes them more useful.

Isaiah 61:1 (NKJV)   "The Spirit of the Lord GOD is upon Me, because the LORD has anointed Me to preach good tidings to the poor; He has sent Me to heal the brokenhearted, to proclaim liberty to the captives, and the opening of the prison to those who are bound;"

2. Ineffectiveness in leadership

The measure of our expertise determines the measure of our effectiveness in performance and production, according to our diligence or laziness in life. We are what we want to be and we'll never become what we don't want to be. Everything in life is a matter of choice.

Education is costly, but ignorance is more costly. Life is made up of a series of choices we make. Then we live by them and they determine our destiny.

Some choose to be ignorant because they are lazy. They have lazy minds and lazy bodies, which produce lazy lives, wasted years, foolishness, and regrets.

He who thinks for himself lives. He who lives by the thoughts of others only exists. A mind is a tremendous potential to waste.

Lazy son squanders father's wealth

A young man gave himself to hard studies and diligent efforts. He did lots of research in the field of his interest and became a multi-millionaire in a short time. He only had one son who was the opposite from him. The son was lazy, careless, untidy, undisciplined, and had no vision or initiative to do anything. He was "mama's baby," and he grew up to be a big baby. He was a total failure in school, at home, and in society.

Unfortunately, his parents died in an accident and suddenly he inherited his father's tremendous wealth. Instead of being fully awakened to become the responsible person to walk in his father's shoes, he began to lavishly spend on himself. In a short time he squandered every penny and died a pauper with broken health.❑

What a difference between him and his father. His father was most effective, while he was useless.

We choose what we want to be every moment of our lives.

Principle	*Comment*
218. Profession without possession among leaders ends up in disastrous depression, which usually affects the people for the worst.	• Superficiality leads to hypocritical living, which reveals wickedness of heart. Hypocrisy is a subtle form of deception —appearing on the outside what we are not on the inside.

Matthew 15:14 (NKJV) "Let them alone. They are blind leaders of the blind. And if the blind leads the blind, both will fall into a ditch."

| 219. A leader who has nothing outstanding to show in his leadership cannot convince others to follow him. | • What we are speaks louder than what we say. Inner determination determines our diligence in what we do. |

Acts 5:38-39 (NKJV) "And now I say to you, keep away from these men and let them alone; for if this plan or this work is of men, it will come to nothing; {39} but if it is of God, you cannot overthrow it; lest you even be found to fight against God."

Principle	*Comment*
220. A leader who thinks people are blind to his actions and unable to discern his qualities, idiosyncrasies, and hidden weaknesses, is fooling himself. He will fail to see his vision implemented without their cooperation.	• We can't fool people without first being fooled ourselves. A leader has to be deceived before he can successfully deceive his people. Deliverance from deception makes a leader realistic and useful.

Matthew 10:26 (NKJV) "Therefore do not fear them. For there is nothing covered that will not be revealed, and hidden that will not be known."

---

221. It is most disappointing to have faith in a leader as a role model and have him turn out to be tainted, setting off a general reaction of sorrow, regret, and anger.	• Wholesomeness of character, where "no part is dark," helps an exemplary leader shine brighter than the sun at noonday.

Titus 2:7-8 (NKJV) in all things showing yourself to be a pattern of good works; in doctrine showing integrity, reverence, incorruptibility, {8} sound speech that cannot be condemned, that one who is an opponent may be ashamed, having nothing evil to say of you.

V. The BALANCE

Where there is balance, there will be stability and safety in the life of a leader, his people, and the whole operation. Some leaders are so spiritually-minded they are of no earthly good. They need maturity to teach them that to be spiritual is to be practical—fulfilling a role in a way that makes deep truth applicable and easily understood.

Revelation without demonstration is unbalanced. Many who receive revelation, in their excitement, fly supersonic, lose sight of the landing strip, and disintegrate in space. A balanced leader has the outcome in view and knows how to reach it safely.

Evangelist obsessed with acquiring glorified body

A popular evangelist had shaken cities by the gift of miracles and a rich anointing that made him a unique orator. One evening after a successful campaign, he became obsessed with the futuristic thought of prematurely acquiring a glorified body, as it is spoken of in the Bible, "we shall all be changed; in a moment, in the twinkling of an eye." (1 Corinthians 15:51-52, nkjv) He established a world church with twenty-four golden pillars, and on each one wrote the name of an elder from a different country around the world.

To my surprise and astonishment, I received a letter from him stating that I had been chosen as an elder from Jerusalem and my name was engraved on one of the pillars. When I awoke from the shock I wrote him a letter assuring him I have not yet attained the state of having a glorified body and please remove my name immediately.❏

I sure wish I had a glorified body, I would save an enormous sum of money on airline tickets, hotel accommodations, and food. I could leave home in the morning to go to any country and return home at night.

Unless a leader is balanced in his views he cannot reconcile the timing of a revelation of a future event with an immediate desire. The excitement of quickened truth throws the immature off balance. Extremism is a form of subtle deception.

A. Followers replicate leaders, for good or bad

As the moon reflects the sun and as children reflect their parents, so followers reflect their leaders. Leaders whose talk is confirmed by their walk will have a great impact on their people. Leaders who contradict themselves and compromise their principles harm their innocent people and must answer to God and man.

Successful operation spans three generations

I have known an operation with three generations. The first generation was a couple who walked with God and served Him with all of their hearts. They published material that was most edifying in its purity of revelation.

They produced a son who followed in their footsteps and took over the operation. He was a success and greatly enlarged the business. In so doing he enlarged the circle of his influence worldwide. He dedicated himself to reproduce himself in others. He has lately handed over the whole operation to one of the followers who proved to be loyal to him and faithful to the call of God upon his life. He had been groomed and approved in character as well as in performance. The man was elated the day he handed over the whole operation to his successor. He trusted him fully.❏

The most successful leader pours out his life into grooming and maturing a successor skillful enough and proven to be capable to assume full responsibility of the whole operation while he is still alive to oversee the transitional period.

We need more leaders who make an impact on the lives of others and reproduce themselves in them.

Principle	*Comment*
222. All replicas should represent the original; it behooves all leaders to be careful how they represent the Lord.	• Our personality is reflected in our performance. Representing God demands the most strenuous discipline in life.

1 Kings 9:4-5 (NKJV)   "Now if you walk before Me as your father David walked, in integrity of heart and in uprightness, to do according to all that I have commanded you, and if you keep My statutes and My judgments, {5} then I will establish the throne of your kingdom over Israel forever, as I promised David your father, saying, 'You shall not fail to have a man on the throne of Israel.'"

---

223. The temperature of a leader determines the temperature of his followers—whether he is cold, lukewarm, or hot.	• Followers are greatly affected by the spirit, attitude, and performance of their leaders on the scale of the Holy Spirit.

Revelation 3:15-16 (NKJV)   "I know your works, that you are neither cold nor hot. I could wish you were cold or hot. {16} So then, because you are lukewarm, and neither cold nor hot, I will vomit you out of My mouth."

Principle	Comment
224. A leader is known to be a failure or a success by watching whether his followers are despondent or joyful, angry or peaceful, frustrated or cooperative.	• Like leaders, like followers. Depth of commitment in a leader touches every cord in their hearts to follow him joyfully and serve him with precision and excellence.

1 Chronicles 15:25-28 (NKJV) So David, the elders of Israel, and the captains over thousands went to bring up the ark of the covenant of the LORD from the house of Obed-Edom with joy. {26} And so it was, when God helped the Levites who bore the ark of the covenant of the LORD, that they offered seven bulls and seven rams. {27} David was clothed with a robe of fine linen, as were all the Levites who bore the ark, the singers, and Chenaniah the music master with the singers. David also wore a linen ephod. {28} Thus all Israel brought up the ark of the covenant of the LORD with shouting and with the sound of the horn, with trumpets and with cymbals, making music with stringed instruments and harps.

B. Leaders must function according to God's plan

Leaders who are taught by the Lord function in the power of His Spirit to fulfill His will and exhort their followers to do likewise. Yielding our lives to the Lord always helps us perform according to His divine pattern and in harmony with His plan.

The leader who has the mind of God and follows His precise directions daily, is bound to succeed when others fail. Only when we do right according to God do we end up right and enjoy a life of fulfillment and full of excitement.

Failing business recovers as son commits it to God

A middle-aged man was called by his father to his office. While in conference with him he was informed that his father's big business was on the rocks because of bad investments. It was hard for the old man to face such a terrible blow. He asked his son to take over the almost bankrupt business. It was very complicated in its operation as it was spread out in different countries. Managing it was even made more difficult because of inadequate personnel.

The son accepted the new responsibility. He went on his knees before God, and thanked Him for his father who had done his best, but failed. His father was a good provider, a loving, affectionate person, and he admired him greatly. He committed himself and the business to the Lord to own and direct him in every decision he was to make.

It was a marvelous recovery. As the Lord began to guide him clearly in every minute detail of this complicated operation, it was not long before the operation recovered and began to show enormous success. This was all due to realizing that self-confidence in a man is God's greatest enemy.❏

The central Scripture in the Bible says "It is better to trust in the Lord than to put confidence in man." (Psalm 118:8, nkjv) Also in Proverbs the exhortation is, "Trust in the Lord with all your heart, and lean not on your own understanding; in all your ways [decisions] acknowledge Him [His lordship], and He shall direct your paths." (Proverbs 3:5-6, nkjv) The psalmist said "The Lord is my shepherd...He leads me." (Psalm 23, nkjv). When we submit to the lordship of Jesus Christ we are bound to enjoy His leadership and His anointing that will make our cup run over with success for His kingdom's sake.

Principle	*Comment*
225. Since spiritual leaders set a moral standard for their followers, they must be held to the highest biblical standard.	• God's ultimate in redemption is to bring us up to His standard, which is Himself. Sin defies God's standard and demoralizes its victims.

1 Peter 1:16 (NKJV)   because it is written, "Be holy, for I am holy."

---

226. Some leaders are able to verbalize what God is doing, while other leaders are able to demonstrate it.	• It takes more discipline to be a demonstrator, and that's what makes ordinary people extra-ordinary leaders.

1 Corinthians 2:4 (NKJV)   And my speech and my preaching were not with persuasive words of human wisdom, but in demonstration of the Spirit and of power;

VI. The BENEFITS of being an Exemplary Leader

An exemplary leader gains the favor of God and the approval of man. Gaining God's favor means that what He appoints He anoints, and what He trusts He entrusts; He reveals Himself constantly. He becomes more real, near, and dear. God advances His cause through exemplary leaders He has tested in the fire of affliction to bring forth the glittering gold that reflects His image and likeness.

Friend and foe alike are compelled to put full confidence in an exemplary leader who becomes a reflector of Christ. He gains the approval of God and becomes a vessel God fully trusts to convey His blessings to the needy. He gains inner stability to keep him steadfast in his pursuit of fulfillment in life. He moves with full assurance of direction. He gains the confidence of others as they behold his uprightness, truthfulness, and transparency. He enjoys their full cooperation, which enables him to gain momentum on his way to reaching his set goal.

It is nigh impossible to enumerate the hidden benefits that surface from time to time as one expands himself to sacrifice for the welfare of others. Some have the "cream" of wealth but are themselves "skim milk." It is far better to BE than to HAVE without BEING. Some people would be worth nothing if they lost everything they have. Becoming a vessel of honor is the greatest honor God bestows upon man.

Tribesman's inspiring example leads to global ministry
God saved a young man from a remote tribe that hunted lions with spears. After his training he entered the ministry full-time. His dedication to the Lord and deep commitment to walk and serve Him made him an inspiring example to his people. God helped him to win many whom God used greatly. God enlarged the circle of his ministry until it became international in scope. He is still reaping great benefits, giving the glory to God.❏

A. Effectively influences people for the Lord

Leaders who are saturated with God's rich anointing have the greatest influence on people for God. As food affects the body and as knowledge affects the mind, the anointing affects the spirit. The richer the anointing upon a leader's life, the more effective he becomes. Their anointing drives the truth into the spirits of their people and affects an eternal change in them.

Samson loses all through foolishness and sin

Samson's only hope to do mighty, miraculous feats was in the repeated phrase in the book of Judges, "And the Spirit of the Lord came mightily upon [Samson]." (Judges 14:6, nkjv) The anointing is God's divine enablement that empowers us to do His will and fulfill His purpose. Every step of wholehearted obedience that stems out of total submission to the Lord, enriches a leader's life with a greater anointing.

We are indebted to the Holy Spirit who is responsible to impart the anointing upon our lives, to make us what we ought to be in God.

It is a sad commentary when the Bible says that Samson, due to acts of foolishness and indulgence in sin, lost the Spirit of God, the anointing of God, and the presence of God. He also lost the position God had given him, his vision, and the confidence of his people. He was finally demoted to the rank of a lower creation to take the place of an animal in the mill. (Judges 16:21)❏

Life's experiences are many, and they vary in their lessons and in their price. Some are more costly than others.

Principle	Comment
227. The godly example of a leader exerts far more influence than any persuasive words.	• Godly living speaks louder in its silence than many audible words—even beyond dynamic words.

2 Corinthians 5:11 (NIV)   Since, then, we know what it is to fear the Lord, we try to persuade men. What we are is plain to God, and I hope it is also plain to your conscience.

Principle	Comment
228. A godly leader walking close to God is contagious to his followers. This explains their cooperative spirit and supportive stand.	• The closer we live to God —and make Him the center of our attraction—the more He shines through us and the more we attract people to Him.

Philippians 2:14-16 (NIV)   Do everything without complaining or arguing, {15} so that you may become blameless and pure, children of God without fault in a crooked and depraved generation, in which you shine like stars in the universe {16} as you hold out the word of life...

Principle	*Comment*
229. When Christ becomes first and foremost in a leader's life, then food, money, position, title, and prestige are secondary, and his example becomes the compelling force that leads others to Christ.	• When a leader gives Christ the preeminence in his life, he makes great strides in his progress toward the full expression of Christ-likeness in his daily life. When Christ is first and foremost, everything falls in its place.

Matthew 6:33 (NKJV)   "But seek first the kingdom of God and His righteousness, and all these things shall be added to you."

---

230. A leader who is a fiery witness is the greatest motivator of men, even among traditionally freezing, legalistic people.	• Where there is fire, there is power. To witness is the calling of everyone, starting with leaders. Every member should be a living witness daily.

Acts 1:8 (NKJV)   "But you shall receive power when the Holy Spirit has come upon you; and you shall be witnesses to Me in Jerusalem, and in all Judea and Samaria, and to the end of the earth."

Principle	*Comment*
231. People grow to love and admire a gentle and helpful leader whose vision is to manifest Christ in whatever situation God places him.	• Only Christ in us attracts people where nothing can ever distract. He is the ultimate of man's fulfillment in life, for time and throughout eternity.

1 Thessalonians 5:14-15 (NKJV)   Now we exhort you, brethren, warn those who are unruly, comfort the fainthearted, uphold the weak, be patient with all. {15} See that no one renders evil for evil to anyone, but always pursue what is good both for yourselves and for all.

---

232. Conformity to Christ changes one's harshness into tenderness and lethargy into activity. What a blessing to be under such a leader.	• The joy of becoming like Christ is a leader's greatest delight in life. His divine qualities become evident in his conduct.

2 Corinthians 4:10-11 (NKJV)   always carrying about in the body the dying of the Lord Jesus, that the life of Jesus also may be manifested in our body. {11} For we who live are always delivered to death for Jesus' sake, that the life of Jesus also may be manifested in our mortal flesh.

Principle	*Comment*

233. The more a leader gets hurt by people, even the ones he has helped the most, the more capable he becomes at helping the hurting, through his sensitivity to what they are going through.

• It is far better to receive many injuries than to give them. We can only help others to the measure that we feel their hurts and empathize with them.

2 Corinthians 1:3-4 (NKJV)   Blessed be the God and Father of our Lord Jesus Christ, the Father of mercies and God of all comfort, {4} who comforts us in all our tribulation, that we may be able to comfort those who are in any trouble, with the comfort with which we ourselves are comforted by God.

234. Opportunities abound to cheerful leaders because they lift up people's spirits by their example.

• Putting the lights on makes all the difference, especially at midnight.

2 Chronicles 7:10 (NKJV)   On the twenty-third day of the seventh month he sent the people away to their tents, joyful and glad of heart for the good that the LORD had done for David, for Solomon, and for His people Israel.

Principle	*Comment*
235. A joy-giving leader is a joy-living leader. He is a joy to live and work with.	• Some leaders are joy-exporters, others are joy-importers depending on whether Jesus is Lord of their lives.

Psalm 5:11 (NKJV)   But let all those rejoice who put their trust in You; let them ever shout for joy, because You defend them; let those also who love Your name be joyful in You.

---

236. Sunshine leaders shine everywhere they go and make the way clear for their followers.	• Living close to Christ saturates a leader with His glorious presence and rich anointing.

Proverbs 15:15 (NKJV)   All the days of the afflicted are evil, but he who is of a merry heart has a continual feast.

B. Produces dedicated followers

A leader who enjoys a sweet relationship with the Lord will reproduce the same in his people. A leader reaps from others in the same measure he invests in them.

Dedication is the act of people who love and care enough to give all that they are and all that they have. The measure of our dedication leaves a deep impression that lasts until our last breath. Dedication will make us 100% owned of the Lord.

Dedicated leader affects his people, thousands saved

A leader who was totally dedicated to the cause of Christ, affected the lives of his people. They numbered in the thousands. He was pastoring a church in a very large metropolitan city.

Every time he felt led to hold a campaign and invite famous evangelists, his people worked day and night reaching every home in the streets and in the high-rises, both far and near, three times before the campaign started. Several campaigns proved to be great successes because of the dedication of his followers, which reflected his dedication. Thousands of souls were reached for Christ.❑

Truly, like begets like. Nothing touches people more deeply than the depth of dedication of their leader. Lord give us more leaders of such caliber.

Principle	*Comment*
237. The final test for a leader to pass is that he leaves behind him in other men the conviction and the will to carry on his vision with the same burden and the same fire.	• What we leave with others will be our last legacy—the sum total of all that was dearest to us and all that we were entrusted with by God to affect time and eternity.

1 Kings 19:19 (NKJV)   So he departed from there, and found Elisha the son of Shaphat, who was plowing with twelve yoke of oxen before him, and he was with the twelfth. Then Elijah passed by him and threw his mantle on him.

238. A leader who leads the way as a godly example will never lack followers who will be willing to lay down their lives, because they behold his dedicated involvement and self-denying labor of love.	• Total dedication provokes the same in others. It impacts the lives of sincere and observant people and ignites in them the same level of dedication—where there is no hesitation to pay the price.

1 John 3:16 (NKJV)   By this we know love, because He laid down His life for us. And we also ought to lay down our lives for the brethren.

Principle	*Comment*

239. The leader who lives an ordinary life in an extra-ordi-
nary way will be followed
by many ordinary people
who feel comfortable
following him.

• Total dedication generates
an ardent spirit, which
makes a great difference.
It changes ordinary
people into extraordinary
warriors.

Acts 2:42-43 (NIV)   They devoted themselves to the
apostles' teaching and to the fellowship, to the breaking
of bread and to prayer. {43} Everyone was filled with
awe, and many wonders and miraculous signs were done
by the apostles.

---

240. An exemplary leader
commands the respect of
his followers without
demanding it.

• People are searching for
well-disciplined leaders
who are walking examples
to follow.

Matthew 20:25-28 (NKJV)   But Jesus called them to
Himself and said, "You know that the rulers of the Gentiles
lord it over them, and those who are great exercise
authority over them. {26} Yet it shall not be so among you;
but whoever desires to become great among you, let him
be your servant. {27} And whoever desires to be first
among you, let him be your slave; {28} just as the Son of
Man did not come to be served, but to serve, and to give
His life a ransom for many."

Principle	**Comment**
241. The leader who is always out in front, being involved in a practical and wholesome way, will never lack cooperation from his followers.	• Those leaders who are in front, lead; those who are in back, drive with a whip. We herd sheep and drive cattle, but we lead obedient men.

Philemon 1:20-22 (NKJV)   Yes, brother, let me have joy from you in the Lord; refresh my heart in the Lord. {21} Having confidence in your obedience, I write to you, knowing that you will do even more than I say. {22} But, meanwhile, also prepare a guest room for me, for I trust that through your prayers I shall be granted to you.

C. Has long-lasting influence

A leader's character reaches its height when it is cultured, controlled, refined, and disciplined. His consistency in his walk with God leaves an indelible mark on his people that propels them to excellence.

Hit man turned tender pastor sparks a harvest

A criminal, who was a hit man for his gang, was converted while he was in prison. He was groomed well in the Word of God and when he was released, he began to serve the Lord in a different capacity. God finally opened the door for him to pastor a church where the Lord moved mightily in the midst. People flocked to his church to behold the glory of God and the miraculous.

He was tender in his spirit and mellow in his attitude in treating his people. They loved him immensely as he affected their lives and influenced them to bring in the harvest.❏

Principle	*Comment*
242. A righteous leader does not need to have a tombstone erected over his grave; his deeds are his monument.	• Our deeds are our testimony for good or evil; good deeds speak for themselves, even after death.

James 3:13 (NKJV) Who is wise and understanding among you? Let him show by good conduct that his works are done in the meekness of wisdom.

Principle	*Comment*
243. Devout men carried Stephen to his grave, but his influence could not be buried. So is the influence of the lives of devoted leaders who have died to themselves and are alive unto God.	• Their lasting influence affects many generations. It transforms their lives to become useful and a great blessing to others. While the voice reaches the ears, influence touches the spirit, soul, body, and purse.

Romans 6:11 (NKJV)   Likewise you also, reckon yourselves to be dead indeed to sin, but alive to God in Christ Jesus our Lord.

---

244. A godly leader may disappear from the scene, but his far reaching influence will continue on indefinitely.	• People are affected more by their leaders than by anyone else. The influence of a godly leader never dies.

Hebrews 11:4 (NKJV)   By faith Abel offered to God a more excellent sacrifice than Cain, through which he obtained witness that he was righteous, God testifying of his gifts; and through it he being dead still speaks.

Principle	*Comment*
245. The more godly a leader is, the greater is his influence. The more diligent he is, the farther his effectiveness reaches.	• Becoming more like God is becoming a man of God who serves the purpose of God and whose influence is far-reaching.

*Proverbs 13:13 (NKJV)   He who despises the word will
be destroyed, but he who fears the commandment will
be rewarded.*

---

246. The leader who inspires others by his godly example, is the greatest achiever in performance and quality.	• When we are inspired by the Lord we inspire others for the Lord; we captivate people to fulfill His will and purpose.

*1 John 3:16 (NKJV)   By this we know love, because He laid
down His life for us. And we also ought to lay down our
lives for the brethren.*

---

247. A refined leader's disciplined walk with God makes him a powerful example to follow.	• Leaders who pay the high price for refining, will enjoy a life that affects the multitudes.

*2 Peter 1:10 (NKJV)   Therefore, brethren, be even more
diligent to make your call and election sure, for if you do
these things you will never stumble;*

D. Will accomplish much

A leader can go only as far as he can see. His vision becomes his guide to reaching his ultimate goal. A leader will accomplish only to the measure he invests in his followers.

A vision born of God will be anointed and sustained by God for His fulfillment. God always begins by imparting a vision to sincere hearts when He has great plans to fulfill.

Nehemiah rebuilds the walls and gates of Jerusalem

In the Old Testament, we read about a great Jewish leader named Nehemiah. He was a man with a sincere heart and he genuinely cared about the condition of Jerusalem. Nehemiah was greatly burdened. He fasted and prayed for Jerusalem, which was in a state of great disorder and disrepair. The walls were destroyed and the gates were burned with fire. As a result of his fasting and praying, God responded to him by giving him favor with the king, whom he served.

God provided for the fulfillment of the vision by giving Nehemiah three things that he himself could have never acquired on his own. First, God gave him favor with the king so that he gave Nehemiah permission to leave and travel to Jerusalem. Second, God gave him favor with the king to rebuild the walls. Third, God gave him favor with the king so that the king commanded provisions be provided for the project.

The vision in his heart was anointed by God and the fulfillment was sustained by God. As Nehemiah committed himself to the journey and then the labor, God sustained him as the vision took shape in reality.

There were many problems and pressures. The various people groups and leaders around the area resented Nehemiah and were against him by intrigue and by threat of violence. They also wrote lies to the king about Nehemiah. Sometimes the Jews themselves did not do right. They enslaved their own brothers by means of debts that couldn't be repaid.

But God sustained the vision in his heart. With God sustaining him, Nehemiah provided leadership in a positive fashion and accomplished much.❑

Principle	*Comment*
248. A leader who moves his people by his exemplary zeal will accomplish much through their united efforts and spirit of cooperation.	• A leader who forges his way through life's complications with undaunted zeal gets through to his people easily.

John 2:17 (NKJV) Then His disciples remembered that it was written, "Zeal for Your house has eaten Me up."

---

249. The leader endowed with discretion from above is bound to succeed where others have failed.	• Divine wisdom makes all the difference in the life of leaders, especially when coupled with strong discernment.

Proverbs 2:11 (NKJV) Discretion will preserve you; understanding will keep you,

---

Principle	*Comment*
250. An exemplary leader's life is like dynamite producing an explosion in his followers, affecting those who are far and near.	• A richly anointed leader affects lives with unlimited possibilities that supersede the norm. They become bold in fulfilling their mission.

Acts 17:6 (NKJV)   But when they did not find them, they dragged Jason and some brethren to the rulers of the city, crying out, "These who have turned the world upside down have come here too."

Appendix A
Scripture References Used

The following Scripture references are used in this book. The numbers in *italics are principle numbers*, and the numbers in **bold are page numbers** of Scriptures used in introductory text.

Genesis 17:1 **11**
Genesis 41:14 *157*
Exodus 14:13 *26*
Exodus 17:9 *197*
Leviticus 11:45 **11**
Numbers 32:23 **173**
Deuteronomy 11:26-28 **158**
Judges 14:6 **190**
Judges 16:21 **190**
Judges 18:9 *173*
1 Samuel 3:19 *74*
1 Samuel 15:24 *182*
1 Samuel 15:26,28 *214*
1 Samuel 17 **72**
1 Samuel 17:32-36 **73**
2 Samuel 12:13 *100*
2 Samuel 20:4-5 *115*
1 Kings 9:4-5 *222*
1 Kings 15:1-3 *198*
1 Kings 19:19 *237*
1 Chronicles 12:17-18 *85*
1 Chronicles 15:25-28 *224*
2 Chronicles 7:10 *234*
2 Chronicles 10:6-7 *83*
2 Chronicles 10:15-19 *104*
Nehemiah 2:17-18 *63*
Nehemiah 2:18 *44*
Job 23:10 *160*
Psalms 5:3 *186*

Psalms 5:11 *235*
Psalms 18:19 *147*
Psalms 19:7 *31*
Psalms 19:14 *92*
Psalms 23 **187**
Psalms 48:1 **107**
Psalms 51:10-13 *49*
Psalms 57:7 **107**
Psalms 68:6 *187*
Psalms 78:70-72 *8*
Psalms 118:8 **187**
Psalms 139 **25, 213**
Proverbs 2:10-11 *165*
Proverbs 2:11 *249*
Proverbs 3:5-6 **187**
Proverbs 4:18 *33*
Proverbs 12:1 *101*
Proverbs 13:4 *204*
Proverbs 13:13 *245*
Proverbs 14:27 *59*
Proverbs 15:10 *131*
Proverbs 15:15 *236*
Proverbs 15:28 *113*
Proverbs 15:32 *156*
Proverbs 16:18 *189,* **72**
Proverbs 16:23 *70*
Proverbs 17:27 *91*
Proverbs 19:20 *151*
Proverbs 21:5 *90*

Appendix B
Other Book Titles

The following book titles are being developed:

1. The Accountable Leader
2. The Accurate Leader
3. The Affectionate Leader
4. The Assuring Leader
5. The Alert Leader
6. The Amiable Leader
7. The Anointed Leader
8. The Apostolic Leader
9. The Appreciative Leader
10. The Ardent Leader
11. The Assuring Leader
12. The Attentive Leader
13. The Authoritative Leader
14. The Balanced Leader
15. The Challenging Leader
16. The Charismatic Leader
17. The Charitable Leader
18. The Committed Leader
19. The Communicating Leader
20. The Compassionate Leader
21. The Concerned Leader
22. The Conscientious Leader
23. The Consecrated Leader
24. The Consistent Leader
25. The Contented Leader
26. The Courageous Leader
27. The Daring Leader
28. The Decisive Leader
29. The Dedicated Leader
30. The Dependable Leader
31. The Determined Leader
32. The Devoted Leader
33. The Diligent Leader
34. The Discerning Leader
35. The Disciplined Leader
36. The Earnest Leader
37. The Efficient Leader
38. The Eloquent Leader
39. The Encouraging Leader
40. The Enduring Leader
41. The Energizing Leader
42. The Enthusiastic Leader
43. The Ethical Leader
44. The Evangelistic Leader
45. The Excellent Leader
46. The Experienced Leader
47. The Faithful Leader
48. The Faith-ful Leader
49. The Fatherly Leader
50. The Fervent Leader
51. The Flexible Leader
52. The Forgiving Leader
53. The Forthright Leader
54. The Friendly Leader
55. The Generous Leader
56. The Goal-Oriented Leader
57. The Godly Leader
58. The Gracious Leader
59. The Healthy Leader
60. The Honest Leader

61. The Honorable Leader
62. The Humble Leader
63. The Industrious Leader
64. The Innovative Leader
65. The Inspiring Leader
66. The Intercessory Leader
67. The Joyful Leader
68. The Just Leader
69. The Kind Leader
70. The Knowledgeable Leader
71. The Leader of Leaders
72. The Leader With Vision
73. The Liberated Leader
74. The Loving Leader
75. The Loyal Leader
76. The Married Leader
77. The Mature Leader
78. The Merciful Leader
79. The Modest Leader
80. The Motivated Leader
81. The Negative Leader
82. The Noble Leader
83. The Obedient Leader
84. The Organized Leader
85. The Pastoral Leader
86. The Patient Leader
87. The Peaceful Leader
88. The Persistent Leader
89. The Polite Leader
90. The Potential Leader
91. The Practical Leader
92. The Principled Leader
93. The Progressive Leader
94. The Prophetic Leader
95. The Prudent Leader
96. The Radiant Leader
97. The Realistic Leader
98. The Refined Leader
99. The Respectful Leader
100. The Responsible Leader
101. The Revolutionary Leader
102. The Righteous Leader
103. The Sacrificial Leader
104. The Scholarly Leader
105. The Seasoned Leader
106. The Secure Leader
107. The Serious Leader
108. The Servant Leader
109. The Sincere Leader
110. The Single Leader
111. The Stable Leader
112. The Stalwart Leader
113. The Steadfast Leader
114. The Submissive Leader
115. The Successful Leader
116. The Teaching Leader
117. The Team Leader
118. The Tender Leader
119. The Thorough Leader
120. The Thoughtful Leader
121. The Trustworthy Leader
122. The Understanding Leader
123. The Unifying Leader
124. The Victorious Leader
125. The Wise Leader
126. The Worshipful Leader
127. The Youth Leader

Appendix C
Psalm 139

Psalms 139 (NKJV)   O LORD, You have searched me and known me. {2} You know my sitting down and my rising up; You understand my thought afar off. {3} You comprehend my path and my lying down, and are acquainted with all my ways. {4} For there is not a word on my tongue, but behold, O LORD, You know it altogether. {5} You have hedged me behind and before, and laid Your hand upon me. {6} Such knowledge is too wonderful for me; it is high, I cannot attain it.

{7} Where can I go from Your Spirit? Or where can I flee from Your presence? {8} If I ascend into heaven, You are there; if I make my bed in hell, behold, You are there. {9} If I take the wings of the morning, and dwell in the uttermost parts of the sea, {10} even there Your hand shall lead me, and Your right hand shall hold me. {11} If I say, "Surely the darkness shall fall on me," even the night shall be light about me; {12} indeed, the darkness shall not hide from You, but the night shines as the day; the darkness and the light are both alike to You.

{13} For You formed my inward parts; You covered me in my mother's womb. {14} I will praise You, for I am fearfully and wonderfully made; marvelous are Your works, and that my soul knows very well. {15} My frame was not hidden from You, when I was made in secret, and skillfully wrought in the lowest parts of the earth. {16} Your eyes saw my substance, being yet unformed. And in Your book they all were written, the days fashioned for me, when as yet there were none of them.

{17} How precious also are Your thoughts to me, O God! How great is the sum of them! {18} If I should count them, they would be more in number than the sand; when I awake, I am still with You.

{19} Oh, that You would slay the wicked, O God! Depart from me, therefore, you bloodthirsty men. {20} For they speak against You wickedly; Your enemies take Your name in vain. {21} Do I not hate them, O LORD, who hate You? And do I not loathe those who rise up against You? {22} I hate them with perfect hatred; I count them my enemies.

{23} Search me, O God, and know my heart; try me, and know my anxieties; {24} and see if there is any wicked way in me, and lead me in the way everlasting.

Appendix D
Your Decision Now Counts for Eternity

All life on earth has a beginning and an ending except man's life. He was created by God an eternal being to live forever. The longing in man's heart to live longer triggered the scientific research for longevity. So far this has been man's quest, but to no avail. The Bible tells us that God "set eternity in the hearts of men." (Ecclesiastes 3:11, niv) That is why within his heart there's an instinctive longing for immortality.

Ever since man's fall in sin he has suffered greatly from a guilty conscience, an oppressed mind, a restless spirit, and a void that nothing in life can fill.

Man is roaming the globe searching frantically for answers in everything he can find for his dilemma, only to sink deeper in his evil ways. That's why Jesus came to offer

1. *Forgiveness of sin*
   "...in whom we have redemption through His blood, the forgiveness of sins." *Colossians 1:14 (nkjv)*

2. *Peace with God*
   "Therefore, having been justified by faith, we have peace with God through our Lord Jesus Christ..." *Romans 5:1 (nkjv)*

3. *Joy unspeakable*
   "...though now ye see him not, yet believing, ye rejoice with joy unspeakable and full of glory:" *1 Peter 1:8 (kjv)*

4. *Love that's eternal*
   "The LORD hath appeared of old unto me, saying, Yea, I have loved thee with an everlasting love..." *Jeremiah 31:3 (kjv)*

5. *Eternal life*
   "And this is the promise that He has promised us; eternal life." *1 John 2:25 (nkjv)*

When we accept Christ as our personal Savior and Lord we enjoy abundant life in our relationship with God as we live to obey Him, do His will, and fulfill His eternal purposes.

Accept Him now and enjoy a foretaste of eternity on earth. You can do this by praying this simple prayer:

> *Lord, I realize I am a sinner and accept You in*
> *my life as Savior and Lord. I love you and desire*
> *to walk with you all the days of my life.*

If you prayed this prayer, then you have become a child of God and His Spirit now lives in you, "Do you not know that you are the temple of God and that the Spirit of God dwells in you?" 1 Corinthians 3:16 (nkjv).

To grow in your relationship with God and to learn His ways...

1. ***Read and obey God's Word daily (The Holy Bible)***
    "Let the word of Christ dwell in you richly..."
    Colossians 3:16 (nkjv)

2. ***Pray to Him***
    "Then He spoke a parable to them, that men always ought to pray and not lose heart..." *Luke 18:1 (nkjv)*

3. ***Fellowship with other Christians***
    "And they continued steadfastly in the apostles' doctrine and fellowship..." *Acts 2:42 (nkjv)*

4. ***Tell others what God has done for you and for them***
    "And we have seen and testify that the Father has sent the Son as Savior of the world." *1 John 4:14 (nkjv)*

As you grow in your relationship and knowledge of God, His Spirit will be working in you to make you like Christ, the ultimate example.